The Manager as an Assessor

The Manager as an Assessor

A Manager's Guide to Assessing
and Selecting People

by Brian O'Neill

The Industrial Society

First published 1990 by
The Industrial Society
Robert Hyde House
48 Bryanston Square
London W1H 7LN
Telephone 071-262 2401

© Brian O'Neill, 1990

British Library Cataloguing in Publication Data

O'Neill, Brian
    The manager as an assessor.
    1. Personnel. Assessment
    I. Title
    658.3125

    ISBN 0-85290-474-6

Typeset by Ace Filmsetting Limited, Frome, Somerset
Printed and bound in Great Britain by Billings, Worcester

Contents

The more intelligent a man is, the more originality he discovers in men. Ordinary people see no difference between men.

Pascal

We succeed in enterprises which demand the positive qualities we possess, but we excel in those which can also make use of our defects.

Tocqueville

Foreword

We are facing a decade of unparalleled competitiveness, where quality will be the watchword and where organisations will be defined by how 'knowledge' intensive they are. New technologies have changed working practices, and European cross-border recruitment will increase dramatically. Moreover, with falling numbers in the workforce, there will be an unprecedented effort to fill the gap through developing the skills of women and of ethnic minorities.

More than ever, managers will need to recruit with skill and sound judgement. This book will help managers to do just that through sensible and systematic steps, and will prove to be an invaluable investment. After all, those companies which will flourish in Europe will do so at the expense of others. Their success will be measured by commitment to quality, customer care, product development and, perhaps most important of all, to their staff, without whom no achievements are ever possible.

Alistair Graham
Director
The Industrial Society

Preface

In the years of working with managers and being a manager myself I was never convinced that personnel assessment was vested with the same importance as most other management duties. Assessing and selecting people were somehow peripheral to the main business of preparing budgets, organising the area of responsibility, keeping the operation on track and generally managing the 1,001 things that come across the desk of a busy manager. And for most managers I knew the task of interviewing a long line-up of job hopefuls to find a single winner was a lot less rewarding than beating the sales target or launching a high-profile marketing drive.

In large organisations it was often left to staffing officers, recruitment specialists, personnel managers, selection officers or inexperienced administrative clerks to handle much of the business of assessment. Certainly the responsible manager would be in at the final interview for the coup de maître but until that point and afterwards he or she would have assumed very little responsibility for what took place. In more extreme cases, it was not uncommon for individual civil servants in the UK to be 'posted' to positions with little if any input or involvement of the managers of those positions. As far as I know this is still the case in some parts of central government.

At least in the private sector those times have been changing. Many organisations are now opting to shift the burden of responsibility for personnel management from staff to line. This book has been written primarily for those line managers who take this responsibility seriously, who wish to follow accepted good practice and who want to win the maximum business advantage from a well-managed assessment function.

Where does that leave the 'old' Personnel department or, to use its more recent title, the Human Resources function? Notwithstanding current predictions about it 'working itself out of a job', I believe the odds of survival and the continuing importance of the personnel function are high, though possibly in rather different ways than before. Less will be required in the way of industrial relations and administration—for the line has now taken on more responsibility here—and more will be expected by way of expert advice and support. This change is already taking place in many organisations. This book is also for personnel professionals, particularly those who are just making a start and need a practical introduction to the subject of personnel assessment.

I would like to hope that there might be something useful in these chapters for the person who feels some discomfort about sitting in judgement and who has questioned what he or she is doing and its impact on other people. Have I made the correct judgement? What have I done to this person's career, feelings and livelihood? What right have I to stand in judgement? Following the best practices in assessment is surely the most reliable and ethical means of ensuring fair and equal treatment.

Being an assessor is only one side of the coin, however, and only one of the reasons why assessment holds a special interest for people in organisations. For as well as being assessors today they might equally be assessees tomorrow. From a more personal perspective most of us have a healthy interest in knowing about ourselves, how we compare with others, how we are likely to be seen by others and how we can put our best foot forward when applying for a job. Gaining some familiarity with the processes and methods of assessment-selection through these pages will help the reader present him or herself to best advantage.

This is a book for practitioners and not scholars. The focus is on what managers need to know (rather than what a psychologist wants to tell them). I have tried in the course of writing these pages to view the world through their lenses. This perspective is, I hope, practical and serviceable. It is not academic. Though I have frequently drawn on the findings of researchers and practitioners, source references have been all but omitted from the text in the interests of having a more flowing 'read'.

As well as selecting material from published work, I have also made extensive use of the practical assessment experiences that I have shared over the years with managers from such organisations as: the Public Service of the Federal Government of Canada; Canadian National Railroads; Ontario Hydro; British Airways; and the Greater Manchester Police. Hopefully these real-world examples will help to give a credible and practical flavour to what may otherwise be seen as concepts that exist only between the covers of a textbook.

Acknowledgements

My thanks to my wife Elizabeth and my friends James McConville and Gerry Moult for their patience in reading and commenting on earlier drafts.

x

Introduction

The chapter topics

Most managers wear two hats: they need to know how to manage assessment and selection efficiently and effectively; and they need to know how to make informed judgements about the people they are going to appoint. Reflecting these two roles the topics fall into two broad and sometimes overlapping categories: those dealing with the planning, organising and controlling of assessment-selection as a management activity and those concerned with the practices of assessment, such as how to conduct an interview.

The process of managing and carrying out assessment and selection activities has its own inherent logic which is reflected in the structure of these chapters. Reading them in sequence will give a sure grasp of the individual steps and the logic of the whole process. Since, in addition, most chapters are more or less self-contained, it is also feasible to dip into any topic of particular interest without necessarily reading its predecessors.

Chapter 1 considers the chief benefits of sound assessment practices to the organisation and to the individual reader. The selection of personnel is an investment decision that demands proper and thorough assessment. Setting assessment criteria and selection standards is the subject of Chapter 2. Every assessment that a manager or a personnel specialist carries out should have a specific job profile against which to evaluate each and every candidate, and this chapter explains how to develop the profile. Chapter 3 explores the various tools of assessment, old and new, that can be profitably used in the assessment process and looks at their relative popularity. Chapter 4 explains how to select the most appropriate techniques and organise them into an efficient programme of assessment that will lead to valid selection decisions.

Chapters 5 and 6 are concerned with 'the selection interview', the first of the two with preparing for it and recognising bad practice, and the second with actually doing it and overcoming any problems on the day. Interviewing receives more space than any other single topic for good reason: it is the most widely used but badly practiced method of assessment and it is the one that can be most readily improved. The subject of Chapters 7 and 8 is objective testing: psychological tests of ability and aptitude, skill and knowledge tests, performance or 'work sample' tests, and personality questionnaires. Chapter 7 describes the main types of tests and questionnaires and Chapter 8 provides guide-lines for choosing and using them. Chapter 9 is devoted to a relatively novel and powerful method of assessment, the 'assessment centre'. This method consists of several individual and group exercises that simulate important aspects of the target job. It has considerable benefits for developing participants as well as for selection purposes.

Chapter 10 draws attention to the need for role clarity and partnership between line managers and staff specialists. Role shifts and the necessity for trained resources are highlighted.

A systematic view of assessment-selection in the larger context of an organisation's human resourcing system is presented in Chapter 11. Evaluating the process and the results of assessment-selection is a critical part of this system covered in the chapter.

In conclusion, Chapter 12 addresses important first principles in which to ground assessment and selection; and a checklist for auditing the assessment-selection activity.

The Appendices

Appendices 1–3 offer some practical guidance and lists for analysing jobs and developing assessment criteria. Appendix 4 gives details of the sources quoted in the text and a bibliography that expands on some of the important topics covered in the text. This bibliography is heavily weighted towards readily accessible British sources. Appendix 5 furnishes details about suppliers of tests and other assessment tools, consulting occupational psychologists and useful professional bodies in the UK.

Language and gender

Readers will find the masculine pronoun used most often throughout the book. In earlier drafts the usual conventions for de-sexing the language were tried but these quickly became laboured and unreadable. Any offence this may cause is unintended and regretted. Like so many before it is my hope that this invidious bias in the English language will soon be corrected once and for all.

Terminology

The field of personnel assessment does not lack its share of specialist terminology and it is difficult to avoid the use of terms which may sound like jargon to many ears. I have tried to use such terms only when they illuminate and have stayed clear of esoteric expressions that would not add very much to the reader's understanding.

To assist readers to find their way through these pages with some comfort it will be useful to have some of the more commonly used terms explained. The words 'recruitment', 'selection' and 'assessment' are terms which tend to have overlapping meanings that may cause some confusion.

By 'recruitment' I mean all of the activities involved in attracting job applicants, getting them to the place of assessment and bringing them into the organisation once they have been selected. Recruitment is concerned with knowing the labour markets and supply, organising advertising campaigns to suit the prevailing market conditions, caring for candidates and managing the flow of candidates.

'Assessment' refers to the activities and methods involved in evaluating an applicant's suitability for the job. Assessment is about defining the qualifications and qualities to look for in candidates, interviewing them and giving them psychological tests and other forms of evaluation.

'Selection' is a process of deciding which applicant or applicants to accept and which ones to reject. Selection decisions are taken during and, most significantly, after the assessment has been completed.

All three words, recruitment, assessment and selection, may be applied to applicants from outside the organisation—external candidates—or to those from within—internal candidates. 'Promotion' is the result of selecting an internal candidate for a higher-level position. Internal recruitment may take place in an open-market system in which job vacancies are publicly posted or advertised in an in-company newspaper or similar organ. Alternatively, an organisation might have a closed policy for internal recruitment whereby the promotion of individual employees is entirely at the discretion of management. 'Succession planning' is typically a management-driven system. People may be assessed in any of these circumstances. This book is primarily about assessment and selection.

Did you know that . . .

- most interviewers form their opinions of a candidate in the first few minutes then look for reasons to justify those first impressions
- the interview is the most popular assessment technique but one of the least reliable
- interviewers generally give significantly higher scores to candidates they like and candidates they judge to be most similar to themselves
- according to one estimate, up to one fourth of all job applications made in the United States are misleading. Applicants for senior management positions are the worst offenders
- it has been estimated that 84 per cent of employers in Britain never use psychological tests and 78 per cent never use personality questionnaires
- even though it is widely used for short-listing, the job applicant's level of general education provides little or no indication about later performance on the job
- personality and skill tests are now being used by some companies to help select manual workers who are flexible, able to work in teams, and have an aptitude for learning new tasks
- despite moves towards European deregulation, in the late 1980s only 5 per cent of the executive directors of British companies were nationals of continental European countries. Thirty three per cent had no international business experience.

1 Why assessment and selection?

Key points

- *The costs of investing in sound assessment practices are inconsequential compared to either the monetary advantage of making accurate selection decisions or the expense of making wrong ones.*
- *Using good assessment practices improves selection and the utilisation of available manpower resources in times of supply shortage.*
- *During times of recession selecting the best top managers is crucial for survival and success. When staff are being shed objective assessment also helps to identify those who are least dispensable.*
- *The globalisation of business and cross-border recruitment demands the selection of people who thrive on cultural diversity, handle complexity with ease and have a wide breadth of vision. Practitioners of assessment must be comfortable on both sides of different borders.*
- *Planning for any significant expansion or change, such as a new venture or a takeover, should include a realistic appraisal of current management's strengths and weaknesses.*
- *Assessment and selection are straightforward processes that involve know-how, commitment and a number of sensible and systematic steps.*

Getting it right first time

Having the right people in the right jobs at the right time is unquestionably one of the keys to any organisation's success. This is equally true for service and manufacturing industries, for utilities and for the public as well as the private sector. It is people that make the difference particularly in organisations that produce and sell high quality goods and services. In the travel business for instance, where there is little to choose between the aircraft of different airlines, it is the service provided by the staff on the ground and in the air that makes the difference to the customer. It is the supermarkets and retail stores which have helpful, service-oriented staff that command the highest profits. On the manufacturing side, whether high or low technology, the production of high quality goods on time and to the customer's requirements demands a work force of skilled and motivated people.

Picking and retaining high-performance managers and employees is the primary objective of assessment. This is what makes it an indispensable tool to managers and gives their organisations an obvious edge over competitors. Assessment is not only the means of recruiting the right people into entry-level jobs; it has a number of other important business applications and implications that warrant the attention of managers in all organisations.

Financial benefits and costs

Managers are sometimes disinclined to go much beyond a 40-minute selection interview because of the overhead costs of developing, purchasing and using more sophisticated forms of assessment. Little thought is given to the real contribution that assessment can make to business profitability. By way of illustration consider the scenario of a computer distribution company with 1,500 employees and average annual sales per employee of £80,000 where new and valid assessment practices have very recently been introduced and are now being used to select employees. The average cost of assessment per employee is, say, £250 and the net improvement in the quality and performance of staff is 2 per cent. Assuming further that this improvement is reflected in the sales figures, the average annual gain would be £1,600 per employee and when aggregated across employees, almost £2.5 million. If the average employee remained with the company for five years, the value of the new system of assessment would be £12.5 million in improved sales, against an approximate initial cost of less than half a million pounds. By introducing better interviewing practices, valid psychological tests and other assessment innovations, gains much greater than this are well within the bounds of possibility.

Making a bad selection decision is often ruinously expensive for it may well include original recruitment and relocation costs, the costs of lost sales and opportunities, the costs of shedding an unsatisfactory person and replacement costs. Taking the above example, the negative impact of poor assessment and selection on the balance sheet could easily be of similar magnitude to the potential gains.

How much is it worth?

Designing and running an assessment programme is costly in direct expenditures and managerial and staff time. Provided that the methods used for assessment are valid, however, the pay-back may greatly exceed the costs.

An assessment centre is used to select senior police officers for a Senior Command Course at the National Police College, Bramshill. Candidates who do well in the centre also tend to do well in the course, and vice versa. Successful completion of the course almost always leads to career advancement. The total annual cost of running the centre is £101,000.

Using utility analysis, Home Office psychologists have been able to show a conservatively estimated net benefit for the centre of £2.19 million. Utility benefits of this kind are computed from the estimated value of the above-average candidate to the organisation, the length of time he or she is likely to remain, and the number of candidates selected.

Selecting people in a tight market

One of the few certainties in an uncertain future is the decline in the supply of young people coming into the job market. By the end of the 1980s many organisations were starting to feel the pinch particularly the civil service which was finding it difficult to attract graduates in the quality and numbers it had come to expect. By the mid 1990s the current decline in the numbers of school leavers will translate into a sobering 25 per cent drop in the numbers of new entrants. Other economic events will undoubtedly influence the strength of this demographic shift but the main impact is now being felt in every sector and will almost certainly continue to be felt through the 1990s. Perhaps the most serious impact of the demographic time bomb will only become apparent as its effects move up the organisational hierarchy to shrink the supplies of professional and managerial talent at more senior levels.

Yet another supply issue is the shortage of personnel with the skills needed in the industrial and service sectors. In high-tech businesses, for instance, organisations are already meeting with, or can expect to have, difficulty finding experienced professionals. This is clearly a sector where supply shortages will bite deeply. According to one estimate, up to 100,000 additional information technology professionals are required over the next five years. More than with any other industry the effect of the shortages will 'knock on' to other industries whose primary business is not high technology, but which rely to a large extent on high technology systems and services to remain competitive.

There is no single answer to these supply problems and the range of solutions being tried is limited only by managers' imagination: expanding into non-traditional labour markets, boosting available training, escalating salaries, using recruitment practices that are more candidate-friendly, offering loyalty bonuses and other perks. But managers will find that the techniques of personnel assessment can help in several ways:

■ Lowering selection standards is a common knee-jerk response to manpower shortages, but this runs the risk of recruiting incompetent people and leaving the organisation with unsatisfactory employees once the shortage corrects itself. In order to reduce these risks it is vital to specify the qualifications, abilities and personal qualities that are required in that job. Procedures for analysing jobs and profiling the required abilities, skills and personal qualities are described in Chapter 2. Defining the job requirements in an objective way provides information for deciding which qualities are dispensable, which ones can be brought up to standard through training and which ones are truly critical. Some compromise is allowable on other criteria but not on the critical ones.

■ Organisations that are planning to extend their recruitment into non-traditional markets will find that mental aptitude tests provide one of the best indicators of a person's ability to grasp new concepts and learn new information and new skills. Other techniques of assessment can uncover hidden talents for leadership and supervision in people who have never had any previous opportunity to display those qualities.

■ Organisations that are experiencing a noticeable decline in the proportion of applicants to vacancies must find ways of making the most of those who do apply. Objective testing and other forms of assessment provide a cost-effective way of gathering a considerable range of reliable and detailed information about applicants in a comparatively short space of time. With information of this kind it is easier to match people with specific abilities and qualities to the jobs that require them. This can be helpful in at least two ways, first by helping to reduce the risks of making an unsuitable selection, and second by reducing wastage in applicants.

Assessment in hard times

On the face of it, the last thing a beleaguered manager needs in an economic down-turn is advice on how to select the best talent, yet paradoxically that may be the time when it is needed most. Here are two examples:

■ A company may need to reduce its costs by shedding staff, but the question arises as to who should go and who should stay? All too often the staff who opt to take redundancy are those who are most capable and best qualified, who can find alternative employment most easily and who are the least dispensable to the company. For organisations with specialist staff or those that have well-developed performance appraisal systems, it is a relatively easy matter to identify the most valued employees. In other circumstances, managers who are faced with the challenge of downsizing would do well to consider the benefits of objective assessment before deciding the specifics of a redundancy policy.

■ Provided that the survival of an organisation is not at stake, the attention paid to making the right top-level appointments should be if anything greater in recession than in better times. The impact of a poor selection decision is clearly going to be much more damaging to an organisation when its margins are tight and the future is in the balance. A company's short-term aim might be, for example, to represent itself in the best possible light so as to make it attractive to potential acquisitors. Here assessment might serve the very useful purpose of identifying the kind of leader who, as the Chief Executive, would be able to improve the company's liquidity and profitability sufficient to attract a reasonable purchase offer. Some people are better than others at battening down the hatches and making a sinking ship salvageable.

International competition

One of the most fascinating business changes that has been taking place in recent years has been the geographic shift from domestic to international markets. More and more companies are competing in the international as well as the domestic arena. In 1988, estimates of cross-border merger and acquisition activity exceeded £56 billion with the UK assuming a leading acquisitive role. This volume can be expected to rise as the European Community rules governing foreign ownership begin to ease further.

Another significant change has been the liberalisation of employment in Europe and the opening up of domestic markets to foreign employers. In the run-up to 1992 and as competition for graduates spirals, several British organisations in sectors as widely different as retailing, computing, accounting and construction have already moved to attract graduates in continental Europe. Whether overseas graduate recruitment will ever reach a significant volume or whether continental employers will be equally interested in British graduates, remains to be seen.

To do business within continental Europe or any other part of the global marketplace, companies must be able to identify people who are able to serve their interests well in different business environments and in different cultures. They must be able to appoint international managers who are capable of handling a great deal of complexity, uncertainty and differing national and cultural perspectives. Their international managers must have a breadth of vision that transcends national boundaries. Boardrooms will become increasingly multinational and directors will be required to work effectively and harmoniously in this diverse environment. All of these requirements, whether at the level of the entry-level graduate or at more senior levels, call for management expertise in assessment and selection.

Determining strengths and limitations

Business acquisitions and joint ventures is another area in which it is important to have a capability for management assessment. Mergers and takeovers represent major opportunities, but only if there are adequate strengths in the new management team to manage the transition and exploit the pooled resources and markets. The challenge of merging two companies, while at the same time maintaining the level of their ongoing operations, demands unusually sure-footed management. The failure of many such ventures to live up to their initial promise must be, at least, partly attributable to individual and collective limitations of management. Taking stock of the strengths and weaknesses of the managers who would be expected to make it happen should, therefore, be part of the preparation for a merger or takeover.

On the other side of the takeover coin auditing the management resource of a new acquisition through individual assessments is similar to taking stock of its financial worth, physical resources or market potential. Clearly, if this is going to be done it should be done before any new organisational structure is finalised or management appointments made.

Fair discrimination

In the UK screening candidates on the basis of their sex or racial membership is illegal. Discrimination on the grounds of age, religion or physical handicap, though not illegal, is unacceptable to many and seems to fly in the face of good business practice. Fairness of employment selection has been widely contested and debated in the courts of the United States and it is there that the most extensive work on the issues has been done. Arvey, an American psychologist and an expert in the field, has given a useful working definition:

Unfair discrimination or bias is said to exist when members of a minority group have lower probabilities of being selected for a job when, in fact, if they had been selected, their probabilities of performing successfully in a job would have been equal to those of non-minority group members.

Arvey, 1979, page 7

Most job applicants and candidates for promotion are prepared to accept being turned down if they feel they have had a fair opportunity to compete and are not subjected to unfair discrimination. However, research into the effects of prejudice in employment has shown, for instance, that non-white people applying for advertised vacancies have significantly less chance of being short-listed than white people regardless of qualifications and abilities.

Sometimes unfair discrimination is entirely unconscious and based on worthy intentions as the example opposite illustrates. Nonetheless, the consequences are exactly the same as deliberate adverse discrimination, and equally damaging. One of the principal causes of unintended discrimination is the failure to apply the principle of *job-relatedness* in assessment and selection.

If a criterion that is used for selecting or promoting people is demonstrably job-related, if it is a genuine requirement of the job, then it discriminates fairly and without prejudice. Selection criteria that are only loosely or remotely related to the job, such as an applicant's general level of education, are more likely to discriminate unfairly against ethnic applicants. Immigrant applicants might be well suited for a vacant job but because they lack an 'O' Level or GCSE certificate they might be rejected out of hand on the basis of their application form.

Good assessment practice is concerned with identifying selection criteria that are genuine, bona fide job requirements and measuring these in a fair and reliable manner.

Apart from any consideration of ethical behaviour, or good corporate citizenship, there are at least two good reasons for

---

A case of unintended discrimination

Until 1980 one of Canada's national railway companies, Canadian National, regularly applied a minimum height standard when it recruited new train crew. The reasoning behind this requirement seemed eminently sensible. When trains were in marshalling yards and industrial sidings, and sometimes on the main line, the train crew were required to climb on and off moving boxcars using a side ladder. As the bottom rung of this ladder was suspended more than a metre above the roadbed this manoeuvre required some agility for a slip could mean a serious or fatal accident. The risk to short people seemed to be unwarranted, hence the height standard.

An unfortunate side-effect of minimum height standards is that they eliminate disproportionately large numbers of women and certain ethnic applicants, and hence are discriminatory. Despite this the railway company was adamant and refused to bend its requirements in the overriding interests of safety.

It took a simple case to change the practice. In the annual recruitment round, one of the applicants was a 'hogger' whose job it was to drive locomotives around the marshalling yard. Getting on and off these locomotives was just as much of a physical challenge as the boxcars posed to train crew. The catch was that the hogger was a young woman who fell below the minimum required height and hence was rejected. It was only after she brought a complaint of discrimination that the company changed its policy and dropped the offending standard. In its place there is now a performance 'test' for recruits consisting of a stationary ladder simulating the real thing.

managers to follow assessment and selection practices that are well grounded in the job and discriminate fairly. In the first place, the direct and indirect costs of defending a legal complaint of unfair discrimination can make a sizeable dent in a company's financial resources. And, in the second, the prevailing problems of manpower supply are strong arguments for taking down any unfounded barriers that rule out large segments of society for no good reason.

Reducing complexity

In all of the assessment situations described so far the task facing the manager-assessor is to gain an understanding of what the individual has achieved until now, what the potential is for further achievement, if there are likely to be any future malfunctions and if the 'personal chemistry' will be right within the team.

Fortunately, there is nothing mystical or particularly complex about doing this or about making the right selection decisions. However, it does demand time, thoroughness, know-how and practice. The basic steps are straightforward:

- the decision to employ or promote is first justified by a business case and a realistic expectation of a profitable return
- a broad specification of the organisational objectives—what the job must be able to produce for the organisation—is agreed
- more detailed specifications are drawn up—a profile of the skills, abilities, knowledge and personal qualities that are required to meet the job and the environmental demands—the criteria for evaluating and comparing the candidates
- the best methods affordable are purchased or developed for short-listing and assessing the applicants
- people with the appropriate level of skills are assigned to the various screening and assessment tasks
- the applicants are thoroughly screened, short-listed and assessed
- the selection decision is made as objectively as possible against the established objectives and criteria.

These steps are elaborated and explained in the chapters that follow.

Specifying the organisational objectives of assessment

An organisation's broad objective for assessment and selection is to have the best qualified, most able and most highly motivated talent at a price that allows it to be competitive and profitable for its shareholders. It might in addition have a general corporate commitment to meeting the social goals of equal employment opportunity. Assessment programmes are also intended to achieve one or more specific business objectives, such as:

- to maintain productivity levels by replenishing the existing stock
- to increase market share by increasing the quality or quantity of manpower
- to reduce turnover costs by selecting stayers rather than leavers
- to change the age profile of a particular class or level of jobs in the organisation in anticipation of a high proportion of retirements
- to reduce training costs by selecting people with a higher aptitude for learning
- to select a leader to lead the company out of the wilderness and return it to profitability, or to float or privatise the company
- to introduce new technology by selecting people with the right skills or aptitudes
- to improve the company's record and public image as an equal opportunity employer

In making a business case for an assessment programme it is important to be entirely clear about what it is expected to accomplish, thinking it through and designing an appropriate strategy to ensure that the objectives are met. Why is this assessment project being run? What benefits will flow to the organisation? How accurate do the choices have to be? Would the benefits of increasing the accuracy of the assessments justify any additional costs? What are its short- and long-term effects likely to be on the organisation?

Trade-offs between opposing objectives as well as between costs and benefits may be necessary. For instance, in demand-driven market conditions where manpower supplies are low, it might not be possible to achieve the two objectives of recruiting highly talented personnel and reducing turnover. Different objectives might very well call for different methods or different criteria for selection. Decisions need to be made at the outset to establish the priorities and estimate their costs and probable benefits.

2 Starting with the job and the selection criteria

Key points

■ *The first step in the assessment process is to understand the job to be filled by analysing it and the environment in which it is performed. From the results the required knowledge, skills, abilities and personal qualities can be deduced.*

■ *Some key points about 'job analysis': build on any previous analyses of similar jobs; obtain the separate perspectives of the job-holders, the job supervisor, and the manager; make allowance for future developments and changes affecting the job; use lists of skill and 'competence' descriptions as aids; management jobs require special treatment.*

■ *A 'competence' is a specific ability to get something done. The goal of job analysis is to discover the competences that are the most critical, that are costly or impossible to develop. These are the ones on which assessment must concentrate.*

■ *Allowance should be made for 'compensating competences': an individual's strengths can compensate for limitations so the assessment process needs to look at the person as a whole.*

■ *Setting an objective 'standard' or a 'pass mark' is difficult to do without some bias. It is helpful to develop 'behavioural rating scales' on which levels of a competence are represented by specific statements of behaviour.*

Once a business case and objectives have been established the first step in assessment is usually the one that is least understood and handled least effectively: the process of analysing the job to be filled and developing a person specification. A person specification defines the physical and psychological qualities and qualifications required in the effective job-holder.

Job analysis

Job analysis refers to the procedures for breaking down the demands of a job and its context into their constituent elements, and then deducing what personal qualities the job-holder must have to get that job done under those particular circumstances. These steps follow in sequence, each one building on the preceding ones:

- define the job in terms of its responsibilities, tasks, results or outputs that the effective job-holder is expected to achieve
- describe the most significant aspects of the environment in which the job-holder will have to work
- outline the competences—the knowledge, skills, aptitudes, abilities, and personal attributes—that are required to do the job effectively, or to learn the job, under the specified conditions.

The next step is to convert these into person (or personnel) specifications consisting of:

- 'dimensions' or selection criteria on which job candidates will at some future point be evaluated
- 'selection standards'—the values on the criteria and the points on the dimensions, that candidates must meet to be considered for selection or promotion.

The relationships between these various steps are outlined opposite.

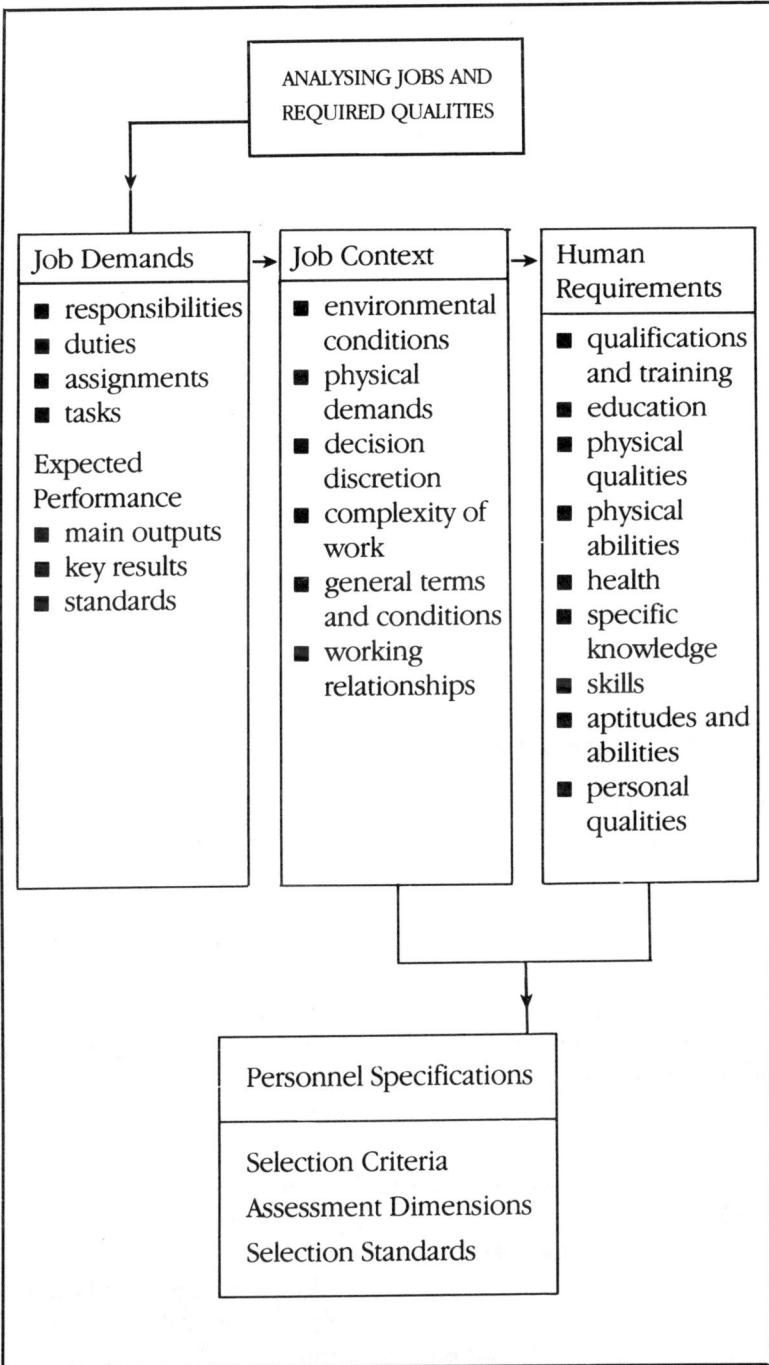

ANALYSING JOBS AND REQUIRED QUALITIES

Job Demands	Job Context	Human Requirements
■ responsibilities ■ duties ■ assignments ■ tasks Expected Performance ■ main outputs ■ key results ■ standards	■ environmental conditions ■ physical demands ■ decision discretion ■ complexity of work ■ general terms and conditions ■ working relationships	■ qualifications and training ■ education ■ physical qualities ■ physical abilities ■ health ■ specific knowledge ■ skills ■ aptitudes and abilities ■ personal qualities

Personnel Specifications

Selection Criteria
Assessment Dimensions
Selection Standards

Costs and benefits

Before analysing a job the first question to ask is how much investment this particular job warrants. A thorough job analysis offers good value for money if the job or jobs in question are senior enough to have a significant impact or are important to the organisation's business strategy, or where there is a sizeable and ongoing recruitment requirement. Less effort is warranted for less important or simpler jobs or jobs for which there is little turnover. Nonetheless some caution must be exercised here for the costs of even one bad selection decision for a junior job, in terms of lost productivity, discipline and morale problems, may greatly outweigh the costs of a job analysis.

For standard occupations that vary little in their job demands, environmental context and human requirements, it is often enough to adapt the results of an analysis done by another organisation.

For those who plan to develop their own job analysis approach, a general method for analysing jobs is given on pages 20 and 21 of this chapter.

Selecting an approach

Job analyses for the purpose of assessment often supply useful data for: job descriptions, a definition of the induction and training needs of new job holders, and job re-design. But a single job analysis cannot meet every need. For example, a job analysis for assessment-selection might not furnish the necessary information for setting compensation levels, and vice versa.

There is no single best way to carry out a job analysis and, indeed, there are half a dozen or more established approaches, each with its own advocates and following. In practice, different conditions and organisational requirements call for different approaches to job analysis.

For example, breaking the job down into lists of tasks is a successful approach for manual and clerical jobs, but not for managerial and professional jobs which involve considerable amounts of unobservable 'mental' work and typically cannot be described well by a list of finite tasks. By contrast, analysing physical demands and environmental conditions is more pertinent to blue-collar and craft jobs. Conducting a large-scale survey using task inventories and ability questionnaires is a highly efficient way to analyse jobs that do more or less the same thing, have a large number of incumbents, and where there is a moderate to high turnover. But for other situations this approach is too mechanical.

As a general rule, it is advisable to use more than one method of analysis to obtain as rounded and as reliable a picture of the job as possible. In planning and setting up the analysis the ways in which the findings should be integrated should be determined at the outset.

Roles and responsibilities

One way of doing job analysis is to observe closely what job-holders actually do, how they do it and how frequently. This can be done by someone in a staff or consulting role. Otherwise the line managers, supervisors and existing job-holders are best able to describe the demands of the job and its context. They are the 'content experts'. As well as seeing the job in a wider context, the owning manager will often know about new technologies or different responsibilities about to become part of the job in the future. Therefore, his or her insights and reactions should be obtained before the analysis begins and after it has been completed.

Involving job holders and supervisors as content experts tends to win support for an assessment project where previously there was opposition and suspicion. Their observations and views from the front line provide valuable information about the realities and practical constraints of the job. If it should happen, as it sometimes does, that the two perspectives are significantly different in any way, this may be a spur to fruitful discussion and research into 'what is this job *really* all about, anyway?'

It is advisable to have someone with no vested interest managing the process of the analysis and keeping it on track. Close as they are to the line operation, managers and supervisors sometimes let predetermined views get in the way of objective observation. Their presence might also cause subordinates to play to the gallery, with consequent distortions of their responses. There is clearly a role here for staff practitioners or consultants, particularly those experienced in fact-finding interviews, to organise and facilitate.

To appear credible, job analysts must be of suitable status.

Senior managers will not believe a junior personnel officer is qualified to interview them to understand what their jobs entail.

Trade-offs and compromises

For purposes of job analysis and assessment, a balance must be struck between treating every job identically—'Anyone who wants a job in this company has to pass the XYZ test'—and treating every single position as wholly unique.

Efficiencies and economies of scale can be gained by clustering individual jobs into job groups or families. For example, all first-level supervisory jobs in a firm might be included in the same broad group if there are only minor variations in the demands, skills and qualifications of the individual jobs. Alternatively, because the jobs are so different, it might be necessary to have different sub-groups and hence different selection criteria for, say, administrative, craft and maintenance supervisors. Or, there might be a core supervisory role that is common to all sub-groups, with unique aspects added on to specific ones. Large organisations would be advised to work out a broad system of job groups and sub-groups to rationalise their assessments.

It should be observed here that the categorising of jobs into bargaining groups or pay levels does not necessarily mean that they are all similar enough to be treated the same way for assessment purposes.

Retaining records

Future analyses carried out in the same organisation will benefit from having a record of earlier projects, particularly what did and did not work. To that end it would be sensible to retain an organised record of the details of the analysis: the procedures used, an account of the job analysis process, the outputs, the reasoning behind any judgements, and the conclusions.

Good documentation may also prove a later justification for the use of a particular selection criterion or standard. Certainly in their defence against charges of unfair discrimination companies in the US have had a stronger case if their records explicitly showed a necessary link between the job and the selection standards.

Positioning for the future

Conventional wisdom recommends a review of a job analysis every two years, more frequently in fast-changing, high technology areas. Conventionally, job analysis looks backwards at the job and environment as they were. It is important to add to it an informed view of where the organisation is going and how it is likely to be affected by future domestic and world events. To neglect the future is to risk appointing people who fit only yesterday's requirements.

The position of the company chairperson is a case in point. At a time when hostile takeovers and management buy-outs have become commonplace, the chairperson of today's Board must be competent in ways never envisaged for his or her predecessors. He or she must now as never before juggle short-term returns and long-term interests, keep the City happy, be expert in sources of capital, and be able to marshal his or her forces and guile to defend against or initiate takeover bids. This point is nicely made in Hugh Parker's *Letters to a new chairman*.

Identifying the human requirements

When the job and its environment have been described in detail it is a relatively easy matter to agree the required physical abilities and the 'hard' knowledge, behaviours and skills. A list of broad skills of this sort is given in Appendix 1. It is less easy to understand what the less palpable aptitudes and abilities are, particularly as different people will use different abilities to achieve similar goals. Making informed guesses about the underlying personality traits is even more difficult to do. In this case it may be useful to consult a practitioner who is well versed in human competences and is able to draw on the experience of others and the evidence of psychological research. Care should be taken to avoid assessing people on characteristics that may be only remotely related to the job.

Using existing lists

The job analyst must make a decision whether to devise from scratch a unique list of personal qualities or competences tailored to the particular job, or to use a set of general competences or skills that have been found to work by other practitioners. The use of generalised competence definitions is an efficient and reasonably successful way to proceed provided they are adapted to the specifics of a particular assignment. Though they are neither definitive nor exhaustive, the lists of skills and competences in Appendices 2 and 3, on pages 161–171, give the less experienced job analyst a useful start.

A general method for analysing jobs

The following outline for doing a job analysis can be developed and adapted to suit the organisation's unique needs and resources.

Step 1 If unfamiliar with the job, the analyst interviews the job supervisors to grasp the main purpose, content and context of the job. He finds out if there are any special sub-groups, which have their own particular skill requirements in addition to the common ones, that should be included in the analysis. He tours the shop floor or work stations to get an overall view of the operation and working conditions.

Step 2 The analyst seeks out and studies documents pertaining to the job—operating manuals, job descriptions, training materials. He becomes familiar with the technologies, the customers, the nature of the industry.

Step 3 The analyst decides who to approach for expert information about the job—job-supervisors and/or job-holders—and how many. He identifies the sample to ensure a good representation, if necessary consulting with unions, and organising the venues.

Step 4 He designs interview guides, task lists and/or survey questionnaires to structure the gathering of data and also for recording in writing the results of the analysis. The lists and forms presented in Appendices 1–3 provide some ideas that can be adapted to suit the assignment.

Questionnaires are an efficient means of capturing the views of a wide range of individuals; but they are time-consuming to distribute, log in, tabulate and analyse. It is important to trial a questionnaire before going live. Inevitably the instructions for completion that are crystal clear to the designer will be mis-interpreted by respondents.

Interviews do not permit such a large sample, and can be more complex to digest, but give a more in-depth insight. In the interviews, a predetermined format is followed without unnecessarily restricting the respondent's freedom to elaborate in his own words. Detailed notes should be taken.

A workshop format works especially well when it is designed to combine the use of questionnaires and/or task lists with group discussion and evaluation.

Step 5   The analyst determines how the data observations are to be integrated and analysed, and prepares sheets for coding and summarising the data. In particular, he thinks out in advance how the human qualities required in the job will be deduced from the analysis of the job demands and context.

Step 6   Using the planned methods and tools, he gathers views and perceptions about the job.

Step 7   He tabulates the data on the pre-formatted sheets.

Step 8   The analyst drafts descriptions of the chief job demands, the context of the job and the required qualities.

Step 9   The analyst distributes copies of the job analysis report to job experts and/or management for review, further evaluation, confirmation, editorial comments and additions. Following this up with face-to-face discussions of the results is often useful.

Step 10   He integrates the feedback into a final job analysis report.

Analysing managerial jobs

In some organisations the world is sometimes turned on its head: the jobs of junior managers or workers are rigorously analysed and assessed while important senior positions are handled informally. Top management often seem unwilling to involve lesser mortals in the specification process. Headhunters and selection consultants frequently collude in this by working to superficial and inadequate briefs. It is in the manager's best interest to ensure that this does not happen.

Because individual managers place their own unique mark on the job, because of the discretion involved in how results are achieved, and because much of the job involves implicit thought processes rather than overt behaviour, the analysis of managerial jobs poses a particularly complex challenge.

The job and its context

Critical questions that should help guide the analysis of managerial jobs are presented below. A form for recording the answers to these questions and other details is presented in Appendix 1, pages 157–160.

1 What are the main purposes and responsibilities of the job as seen by the responsible manager, subordinates, the customers, other managers?

2 What key outputs does the job supervisor expect from the job holder, this year, in the future? Do others expect anything different and what?

3 Has the job existed for some time or is it new? If new, what are the problems and opportunities involved in shaping the job?

4 What is the potential impact of the job and its incumbent on the success and survival of the organisation?

5 What is the climate of the organisation, what are the cultural values that the incumbent must adjust to?

6 What are the vertical relationships, with superiors and subordinates, what horizontal working relationships with colleagues and other departments? What issues and relationships have to be positively managed?

7 Are there suppliers or customers from outside the organisation to whom the job-holder must relate?

8 Are there any particular physical demands or hazards with which some managers might not be able to cope?

9 Are there any other job aspects that are likely to place pressure on the successful candidate?

The concept of 'competence'

'Competence' is a word now much in fashion. It denotes an ability to perform the duties, fulfil the responsibilities and achieve the outputs that collectively make up a particular job in a particular company. To be a successful computer salesperson an individual needs to have a set of particular competences in order to sell lots of computers.

The reader might find it convenient to think of a competence as a bundle of separate but interacting elements. Suppose that one of the competences our salesperson must have is 'getting a foot in the door' of potential corporate clients. The elements of that competence might be:

■ moderately high self-confidence—to make cold calls, to state a position convincingly
■ a positive outlook—to be able to keep on making cold calls and mailing brochures, to look for leverage in even adverse circumstances
■ better than average verbal reasoning—to explain the complexities of computer applications to non-technical managers
■ a high level of adaptability and resilience—to adjust tactics or style to different clients as markets change or as competitors introduce better products
■ a superior knowledge of competitive products and their relative strengths and weaknesses.

Knowledge, skills, abilities and other personal qualities are the elements of competence. Individual competences are also expressed in behavioural terms, which can all be quite confusing to the newcomer to assessment. The important thing is to work with clear, agreed and, hopefully, reasonably simple definitions of what is intended.

The critical competences

Analysis of a job and its competences often produces an unrealistic wish list. Some few of the identified competences will be particularly critical and need to be highlighted but others can be discarded with no great loss. Isolating the few most critical job competences is commonly done by:

■ scrutinizing the record of the job analysis to check which qualities are *really* essential

- identifying and eliminating the competences that can be brought up to standard through development or training
- eliminating competences that are in high supply and that can be taken for granted in virtually all candidates
- considering known job-holders who are, or were, either excellent or particularly ineffective, and identifying the particular competences that discriminate most decisively between the two. Competences that do not discriminate are discarded.

The results of this final winnowing will isolate the competence dimensions on which candidates ought to be assessed and selected.

Competence compensation

Of course, the more demanding the specification, the fewer the number of satisfactory candidates and the more probable it is that they will already be employed. Experienced managers are, in fact, fully aware of the need to compromise when selecting and promoting, particularly when the supply of people is thin. Their task is to weigh the individual's particular mix of competences, to judge if the strong ones compensate for the weak ones, and to predict the impact on the job and on work relations.

An assessment programme for selecting participants for a fast-track management development programme in British Airways illustrates the point. The aim of this initiative was to develop a talent pool of highly competent managers each of whom would be able and willing to take on senior responsibility in any part of the airline. Candidates successful at the assessment would participate in an in-company MBA programme to develop their abilities to function in general management roles. The cornerstone of the assessment was the list of general management competences, shown opposite, identified through a process of job analysis. The critical task for the managers and the psychologists who were assessing was to evaluate potential from the individual's *balance* of strengths and weaknesses, for few candidates came up to standard in each and every one of the prescribed competences.

Senior management competences

The following list of competences, developed for an in-company high-flier programme at British Airways, is described in greater detail in *The Photofit Manager* (*see* Bibliography).

VISION	The ability to develop innovative, well-formed, coherent and future-oriented scenarios.
DIRECTION	The ability to generate strategies, plans and tactics based on a good assessment of priorities, facts, risks and possibilities.
BUSINESS ORIENTATION	A business attitude and business sense that permeates every decision and action.
RESULTS ORIENTATION	The drive to be in command, to have responsibility and achieve results, and to champion worthy causes.
MANAGING RELATIONS	The personal qualities and interpersonal skills that promote open and constructive relations with superiors, subordinates, peers and people outside the department.
RESOURCE MANAGEMENT	The ability and skill to determine needs and manage the acquisition and deployment of resources, both human and physical, in a business-like way.
LARGE ORGANISATION PERSPECTIVE	An appreciation of and sensitivity to the complex interdependences in the world's largest international airline.

This complex interdependence and compensatory nature of human capabilities has an important implication for competence-based approaches to assessment, selection and development. Even though the process of specifying and defining the critical competences of a job should be done rigorously and in a structured fashion, and almost inevitably will be expressed as a list, assessors should not lose sight of the humanity of the candidate. He or she is a unique and complex whole, not reducible to a set of pluses and minuses on a page of competence descriptions.

Resisting temptations

Resist the temptation to skip the job analysis and get straight into the task of specifying the qualifications and qualities desirable in the successful candidate. While better than no specification at all, this runs the risk of producing impossibly high specifications for a superman or superwoman, while overlooking one or more of the key requirements for the job. It might also lead to the specification of wrong criteria and the placement of square pegs in round holes.

Selection standards and rating scales

Probably the single most intractable question in the art of assessment is how to set a standard or cut-off for selection and rejection. With the exception of physical characteristics—height, weight, age—and trade, technical or professional qualifications or a professional degree there are no absolute standards for making selection decisions. Indeed, objectivity by itself, without any proof of job-relatedness, is not enough. Age, for instance, gives no assurance of competence even though it appears in more than 80 per cent of management job ads in UK newspapers and is widely used to screen out candidates early in the selection process.

To bring a degree of objectivity to the judgement of the assessor, psychologists over the years have researched and devised different ways of developing 'rating scales'. The general idea is to have a linear scale for each dimension of competence which assessors can use in interviews or in an assessment centre to assess and evaluate candidates.

Three of the more widely used scales are shown opposite: a numerical scale, a descriptive adjective scale and a behaviourally anchored scale. The competence of oral communication is used for illustration. The numerical scale and the adjective scale share the same advantages: easy to construct, easy to score and are easy

Competence: oral communication

Numerical Scale:

```
   1    2    3    4    5    6    7
   ┌────┬────┬────┬────┬────┬────┐
  low        average        high
```

Descriptive Adjective Scale:

```
   ┌──────────┬──────────┬──────────┬──────────┐
inadequate  poor    average   good    excellent
```

Behaviourally Anchored Rating Scale:

— 5 Speaks understandably regardless of circumstances. Explains complex concepts without difficulty. Always uses proper terms, expressions. Understands readily what others are trying to communicate.

— 4 Speaks easily and gets his or her message across accurately and fluently. Listens attentively, understands and confirms his or her understanding.

— 3 Exchanges thoughts and information in a clear, understandable manner. Gets directly to the point. Listens and understands most of what was said.

— 2 Sometimes fails to get his or her message across. On occasions must be asked to repeat or clarify. Occasionally forgets to acknowledge message or await a reply.

— 1 Consistently unable to convey information orally. Says too little or too much. Never checks to see if his or her message was received correctly.

to describe and evaluate statistically. They also share the same disadvantages. Assessors have difficulty agreeing on the meaning of the points on the scales because they are not defined in concrete terms; they are not used to thinking what a '1' or a '7' in oral communication means. Consequently rating judgements on scales of this sort tend to be unreliable.

Behavioural scales

Behavioural rating scales are the most robust. Assessors have little difficulty understanding and agreeing their meaning and they are relatively free from the typical biases that creep into assessments. Inexperienced and untrained assessors can use these scales effectively with comparatively little training. Their disadvantages: they are relatively difficult and time-consuming to construct; and the rating process takes more thought, and therefore, more time.

The behavioural statements that ' anchor' these scales are drawn from the material gathered during the job analysis. Strictly speaking, the process for developing 'behaviourally anchored rating scales' is a lengthy one. In practice, experienced practitioners usually do this more simply by adapting or composing behavioural statements for the ends and centre points of the scale, checking them out with a few content experts, then developing a final draft.

The ideal number of points to have on an assessment scale depends on :

■ The levels of competence it is useful to differentiate. On certain dimensions for certain jobs two points, yes and no, might be sufficient. For instance, testing if a candidate can lift and carry a piece of equipment weighing 30 pounds. In another situation, several more points on a dimension might be useful for ranking candidates from most to least competent.
■ The ability of assessors to make discriminations on the dimension. Unsophisticated assessors with little training might discriminate three points successfully—unacceptable, acceptable and outstanding—while more sophisticated assessors might be capable of five or seven.

Managers and practitioners are advised to develop behavioural rating scales that are 'anchored' by job-relevant behavioural indicators at least at the two extremes. This gives greater assurance that the assessors will mean the same thing.

The issues of setting standards in interviews, psychometric tests, assessment centres and in making overall selection decisions are considered further in later chapters.

3 The tools of assessment

Key points

- *Application forms and selection interviews are the assessment tools most widely used; psychological tests and 'work sample tests' are used in only a few companies.*
- *Relatively new methods that show particular promise are 'biodata' and 'assessment centres'. Cognitive tests of mental ability also give good value for money. The use of mental ability and personality tests are likely to increase as the intellectual demands of jobs grow and as the work force moves towards multi-skilling and team working.*
- *A number of job-related methods—tests of knowledge, skill, performance and trainability, and the assessment centre —have high levels of credibility and acceptability.*

Assessment methods used

Assessors have two types of tool at their disposal, broadly speaking: those like a psychological test which the applicant takes alone for later scoring and evaluation by an assessor; and those like a biographical interview in which the assessor is actively involved in eliciting information or directly observing what the applicant says and does. Assessment techniques are also oriented either towards past history (e.g., curriculum vitae) or present performance (e.g., a knowledge test).

The most widely accepted and used methods for assessing

people are shown on page 33 and will be discussed later in the chapter. More esoteric techniques like handwriting analysis and astrological prediction, have little scientific support and are not reviewed here.

Application form and curriculum vitae

Application forms are used by virtually all organisations for many kinds of vacancy. They are standardised for ease of completion and for ease of administrative processing. It is helpful to have application forms that are adapted to the special circumstances of different occupational groups—for example new school leavers, graduates, tradesmen, operating staff, clerical and secretarial staff and managers.

This method is most widely used at the initial stages of recruitment to screen out unsuitable candidates and to reduce the number of applicants to manageable proportions. Job applications are given on average about three minutes' scrutiny in the preliminary selection process, so it is vital for application forms to be designed very carefully to capture essential information. It is also used to prepare the assessor for the interview, as an input document for the personnel record and to 'bank' candidates for future vacancies. It should be well designed and printed on good quality paper to promote a positive image of the organisation.

The kinds of information most often sought in application forms are:

- *Identification:* full name, age, address, home telephone number, contact telephone number, date of birth, state of health, citizenship, place of birth.
- *Educational attainment:* qualification and grades, year granted, name of the granting body or institution.
- *Professional and technical qualifications:* qualification and grades, year granted, name of the granting body or institution, membership of professional and scientific bodies.
- *Occupational history:* present and previous employers, dates of employment (including month), chief responsibilities, number of staff supervised, reasons for leaving. Usually for the present and last three or four jobs.

- *Salary history and benefits:* salary in present job, salary in earlier jobs, fringe benefits.
- *Special abilities and skills:* for example languages spoken and written, programming expertise, training skills.
- *External interests:* this can be relevant on occasion, especially for people with no work record such as graduates. Sometimes a useful starting point for a line of questioning in the interview.
- *Reasons for applying:* written in free style this can tell something about writing skill and, again, may provide a useful starting point for subsequent interview questions.

Composed by the applicant the curriculum vitae, or CV, is a self-marketing tool that allows candidates to communicate their achievements and accomplishments to prospective employers. Three common difficulties qualify the usefulness of these two methods:

- candidates tend to 'inflate' their accomplishments and sometimes deliberately deceive
- subjective and idiosyncratic interpretation by those who screen and select. For example some interpret a long period of service with one employer as a lack of drive, others see it as proof of stability and 'maturity'. Some view job movement as a lack of perseverance and others as initiative
- assessors over-interpret the information received and how it is presented. For instance, applications are frequently binned on the strength of poor grammar, spelling or handwriting in cases where these are irrelevant to the demands of the job.

References

References are sometimes taken as a pre-selection screen and sometimes as a final check before an offer is made. They are used to verify information supplied by the candidate and to obtain evaluations of past education or work performance. References may be requested by writing, by telephone, or in person. Referees may be invited to give their written opinions and evaluations of the applicant in free style, on prescribed rating scales or other forced-choice format.

Reference requests suffer from low return rates, particularly writ-

Major tools for assessing people

Indirect observation: self-description or private performance	Direct observation: observed and reported by another party

Past Oriented

Biodata	Personnel records
Personality questionnaire (multiple choice)	Qualifications (education, professional, technical)
Application form	Performance appraisal
Personal history and career interests	Biographical interview
	References
Curriculum vitae	Technical interview

Present-Performance Oriented

Mental ability tests	Job performance tests
Paper-and-pencil skill tests	Trainability tests
	Technical interview
Paper-and-pencil tests of occupational knowledge	Situational interview
Assessment centre (e.g. in-tray test, report writing exercise)	Assessment centre (e.g. group exercise)

ten requests, from leniency—referees are disinclined to give negative evaluations—and from low validity. Some organisations have a policy of supplying only the candidate's dates of employment and nothing else.

Nonetheless, expending effort to obtain thorough references can pay off handsomely. The reference method can be improved by:

- using good interview skills when seeking references by telephone or in person. An otherwise cautious referee will open up to the right approach from the requester. Some of the techniques for interviewing described in chapters 5 and 6 will assist.
- using structured forms with rating scales which tend to give more reliable results than open-ended reports. They are also easier to complete and so more likely to earn a co-operative response.
- using the person's ex-supervisor rather than the personnel department as the information source. The former is much more likely to know that person's strong and weak points.

Biodata

Known variously as the Biodata Form, the Biographical Information Blank or the Weighted Application Blank, this form of gathering historical information about candidates has a relatively recent history and has shown considerable promise. It is an objective, research-based questionnaire designed and tailored to a particular job or occupational group in an organisation. It consists of forced-choice questions about verifiable biographical characteristics. Research is first carried out to identify the background characteristics that are found in good job performers and absent in poor performers. Questions relating to these characteristics are then inserted in a biodata form for future job applicants and an appropriate scoring plan is devised. An example of questions from a biodata form introduced by the Halifax Building Society for recruiting counter and office staff is given opposite.

One drawback is that, having to be tailored to a particular job or group, the biodata method requires the gathering of a great deal of information and a not inconsiderable investment before it can be used. An experienced designer of biodata forms must also be involved. But once developed, it is far more reliable, free from bias and more predictive than less objective methods. It is normally machine-scored by an optical scanner linked to a computer. This permits rapid scoring and calculation of a predictive score.

Questions from the Halifax Building Society Biodata Form

- How many brothers and sisters do you have?
- How much freedom or independence did your parents allow you up to the age of 16?
- What was your highest grade obtained for mathematics at school or college?
- What was your highest grade obtained for English (language or literature) at school or college?
- Please indicate the number of O' level, GCSE, A' level or equivalent subjects passed.
- Have you obtained any qualification through part-time study?
- How did you arrange your revision time?
- How much of the set school or college work did you usually manage to complete on time?
- Which one of the following do you believe contributed most to the level of success you attained at school or college?
- How often did you take paid employment during your final two years at school (e.g., a holiday or Saturday job)?
- Which elements in career choice are most important to you?
- Which types of tasks would be most interesting to you?
- How often do you go out with friends socially or to places of mutual interest?
- Thinking about the hobbies you have now, how did you first come to be interested in them?
- What best describes your approach to planning your work?

From *Personnel Today*, 9 January 1990.

Biographical interview

Known by different names, this form of the selection interview is usually conducted by a personnel officer or a manager. It covers such items as educational history, early social activities, school activities and achievements, current life style and interests, record of employment and training, work achievements and interests, interpersonal working relations, career intentions, citizenship and qualifications to work in the country, mobility and any restrictions on employment or work. Apart from the application form the interview is the most common assessment-selection method in use. A contemporary survey of selection practices in the UK found that over 90 per cent of selection and promotion decisions were based on the interview on its own or the interview with other assessment methods. This survey is described in greater detail on page 41.

Personnel record

Failure to use available talent through lack of current information about skills and experience is demotivating and risks losing good employees to other organisations.

Some organisations are able to make intelligent use of their human resources by maintaining a skills inventory, including employees' educational and training accomplishments, and using this record for positive screening.

A record of poor attendance, frequent sickness absence and disciplinary problems bodes ill for performance in a future job. Therefore information from the official personnel record is also used for screening out internal candidates.

Record of qualifications

General educational attainment should be distinguished from specialised education, and professional, technical and trade qualifications. The latter are manifestly job-related and highly relevant to the selection process, but there is no convincing evidence that general level of education is indicative of an applicant's work competence or motivation. In fact, research has shown only a weak and inconsistent association between general educational attainment and occupational achievement. Given the vagaries of early educational choice, individual differences in young people's attitudes to higher education and the wide social differences in educational opportunity, this is hardly surprising.

Furthermore, the longer it is since a candidate has finished with formal education, the less useful becomes the educational record as an indication of ability. People's motivations change and their values can be re-shaped by life experiences. The individual who scraped through university with a third-class degree might be much more motivated by business than he or she was by an academic environment. Many successful business men and women today, of course, have no qualifications at the tertiary level of education.

Personal history and career interests

A variation on the application form, this method consists of a structured or semi-structured questionnaire to elicit background information from internal staff members as part of their career development. Typically it covers educational attainments, work history, career information and aspirations, training accomplishments, preferred career directions, the individual's readiness to move jobs or place of work, assignment interests and a personal audit of strengths and weaknesses. It is a useful tool for encouraging employees to reflect on the direction their careers are taking and for giving managers added insights into their subordinates' needs, wants and potential. It may be used as an informed starting point for career counselling.

Efficient and economical to design and use, personal history questionnaires are used largely for career development purposes, though they might also provide a useful starting point to an interview for possible promotion.

Performance appraisal

Provided it is done sensibly and reliably the performance appraisal yields valuable evidence for assessment and selection, it is economic and it is efficient.

It has two notable drawbacks:

■ the reliability of performance appraisals is often suspect—

appraisal ratings, more often than not, are affected by positive and negative biases, by the appraiser's liking for the assessee, by an absence of consistent measurement standards and by pay considerations
■ the relevance of the performance appraisal is also questionable if the current job and the target job are significantly different.

Paper-and-pencil test of knowledge

A type of achievement test, this method of assessment consists of objective multiple-choice items that cover the specialist knowledge required in a specific occupation, trade or profession. By way of illustration, a knowledge test for electricians might include a problem involving the reading of a wiring diagram.

Developing such a test requires the expertise of someone with a grounding in psychometrics and test development and a careful analysis of the required job knowledge.

The advantage of this type of test is that it is highly valid, job-related, credible and efficient to administer and score.

Paper-and-pencil skill test

This method of assessment is also an objective test of achievement consisting of objective multiple-choice items. It covers either a basic skill, such as general numeracy or literacy, or specific job-related skills such as clerical filing, coding, checking, spelling and grammar. Commercial tests of clerical skills are readily available, they are economical and are easy to administer and score. Skill tests do not assume any specialised knowledge.

Mental ability test

There are many psychometric tests of mental ability from general intellectual ability to special abilities such as aptitude tests for computer programming and spatial reasoning ability. These are used to determine candidates' aptitudes to learn the job. Again, this type of test comes in an objective, multiple-choice format, is highly reliable and has a high potential validity. It is comparatively inexpensive and gives excellent value for money. Despite these advantages psychological tests are not widely used in the UK, because information on how they can be put to practical use is not readily accessible to most employers.

Personality questionnaire

Personality questionnaires are self-descriptive, their items are true-false or multiple-choice in format, and they provide a comparative picture of how the respondent typically responds to himself, to others and to the world in general. The commercial questionnaires available for assessing personality traits, interpersonal qualities, interests and motivation are legion.

Assessment centre

An assessment centre is a method that involves candidates in several different job-simulating exercises under the scrutiny of several assessors who are usually experienced line managers or supervisors. Exercises range from individual tasks done privately, like the simulated in-tray test, to the leaderless group discussion. An in-tray exercise typically consists of a number of documents and messages similar to those found in a real in-tray. The candidate is required to process the information and indicate what response or action would be taken for each item. Group exercises of many different types are used to simulate work situations that require team work, leadership and group problem-solving.

The assessment centre is a powerful method whose use has started to grow in the last few years. It is highly job-related, gives a rounded, multi-faceted view of the candidate and has high levels of validity and acceptability. The main disadvantage is that it is costly to develop and run.

In-depth psychological assessment

This method is generally reserved for senior appointments at and just below the Board level. A shortened form may be used for middle management appointments. It normally consists of a battery of psychological tests, an intensive interview and a subsequent meeting to give feedback and sometimes career counselling. Psychologists offering this assessment service should be experienced in and understand the world of business and organisations.

The in-depth assessment is particularly well suited to giving a rounded picture of people—their motivation, typical manner of responding under different conditions, visioning capacity, leadership style and preferred roles.

Trainability test

Trainability tests require candidates to perform a task, usually simplified and standardised, that is an intrinsic and important part of the job. They have two distinct stages. In the first candidates are given training on the critical task and in the second they are observed and assessed as they attempt to perform the task. Tests of this kind have been developed for many different trades and for various other jobs. For example, an applicant for an apprenticeship in carpentry might be shown how to make a simple T-joint and then be required to make one himself. Trainability tests are objective, eminently job-related, acceptable to candidates and highly predictive of learning ability.

Job performance test

Also known as work sample tests, this method resembles trainability testing without the training stage. It is used to assess current ability to perform rather than the ability to perform in the future. A standard typing test is a job performance test. They have similar advantages to trainability testing and are highly valid.

Group exercise

Skill in managing teams and handling work relationships is a frequent job requirement for managers, supervisors, team leaders and other staff. A group exercise typically lasts from 20 minutes to an hour. It involves anywhere from about five to eight candidates, with a ratio of management assessors to candidates of two or three to one. Groups of just two candidates are a special case.

The task assigned to the group may be a problem requiring a consensus solution or a discussion of some topic of interest. While some exercises require painstaking design, others can be devised relatively speedily.

This method is good for evaluating skills and abilities in team working, leading others, influencing, negotiating, oral communication, interpersonal sensitivity and decision making. They are quite labour-intensive for assessors.

Popularity of different methods

For the reader who is interested in the current usage of different assessment methods some interesting figures, derived from an extensive survey carried out in the UK by the Institute of Manpower Studies (IMS), are presented on page 42. Other studies would suggest that the IMS figures may slightly underestimate the use of psychological tests, though the evidence is generally consistent with its findings. One of the most telling findings is that psychological tests of mental ability and skill are very rarely used in small and medium-sized organisations, or for manual jobs. With the trends in the industrial sector pointing to increased team working and multi-skilling, the use of ability and personality tests can be expected to grow. A similar change in test usage might also be expected in the service sector with the explosion in 'knowledge work' and the growing use of information technology.

The frequency of use of different assessment techniques in the UK

METHOD	OCCUPATIONAL GROUP							
	Managerial and Professional	Scientific and Technical	Buying, Marketing and Selling	Clerical, Secretarial and Administrative	Manual Foremen and Supervisors	Skilled Craftsmen	Unskilled and Semi-skilled	All
Application form and CV	+	+	+	+	0	0	0	+
References	+	0	0	+	0	0	0	0
Interview	+	+	+	+	0	0	0	+
Psychological Tests	0	0	0	—	—	—	—	—
Trainability Tests	—	—	—	0	—	0	0	—

Key: + = substantial use by 76% or more of the sampled organisations
0 = substantial use by 25% to 75% of the sampled organisations
— = substantial use by less than 25% of the sampled organisations

Abstracted from *Report No. 160*, 1988, by S. Bevan and J. Fryatt of the Institute of Manpower Studies.

4 Organising the assessment programme

Key points

- *Choosing which assessment techniques to use depends on such considerations as: known suitability for the purpose, reliability, validity and acceptability, freedom from unfair bias, cost-effectiveness, and the availability of time and competent staff to administer and score them. These factors should always be considered when designing a purpose-built method.*

- *The reliability of an interview or other assessment tool may be usefully tested by trialling it before using it with real candidates.*

- *Choosing several rather than just a single method of assessment gives a more rounded and dependable picture of a candidate's true potential.*

- *The chosen methods are organised into a sequence of stages or hurdles to make them easier to administer, to screen out unsuitable candidates, and as an aid to the process of making selection decisions.*

- *The number and complexity of the stages in the assessment programme will depend upon the numbers of vacancies and applicants, the candidate/vacancy ratio, the potential impact of the job-holder on the organisation's business, and several other factors.*

- *An assessment day must be orchestrated carefully and scheduled to supply the necessary data for making sound selection decisions while meeting the needs of the candidates and assessors.*

THE MANAGER AS AN ASSESSOR

To assemble a sensible assessment plan, appropriate methods for assessing candidates against the selection criteria have to be chosen or designed in a way that meets the manager's resources and time constraints. In that context, it will be useful to consider here three interrelated aspects of the assessment planning process:

- choosing or designing the most appropriate method or methods
- organising the assessment methods into a logical sequence of stages
- organising an assessment day.

Guidelines for choosing or designing assessment methods

Relative strengths

Different methods are suited to different purposes. The guidelines shown on pages 46–47 give some broad information about the relevance of the methods reviewed in Chapter 3. The number of pluses is a rough indication of how well a method suits a purpose. By way of illustration, cognitive tests, assessment centres and in-depth psychological assessment are highly rated (+++) for assessing intellectual effectiveness. Situational interviews and knowledge tests are rated next most effective for this purpose (++) followed by references, record of qualifications and group exercises (+).

This categorisation is approximate and should not be followed slavishly. In the instance given, the most apt method will ultimately depend on the precise nature of the intellectual requirement.

Reliability

Using a method that gives different measurements each time it is used with the same candidate is a bit like using an elastic ruler. It is unreliable and has no selection value. Reliability is a measurement concept widely used in the psychology of assessment. It refers to the consistency of a method, its capability of delivering the same or similar scores for the same individual at different times and with different assessors.

For example, the reliability or consistency of an interview for a particular job might be tested experimentally by having two interviewers, operating independently, assess and score the same people. That is, every candidate would be interviewed twice, once by each of two interviewers. If the candidates' scores were found to be ranked in more or less the same order by both interviewers, then the interview would be considered reliable.

The reliability of a psychological test is also evaluated by administering it twice to the same persons, or by giving a sample of people two alternate forms of the same test with a period of time intervening. Statistical comparisons of both sets of scores yield an objective numerical measure of the test's reliability.

The more reliable a method the more reason there is to choose it. Only those that give reasonably consistent measurements of candidates' capability should, of course, be used.

Validity

This is another concept of psychological measurement which refers to the degree to which a particular method is able to measure abilities and other qualites that are relevant to job effectiveness. A well constructed typing test is a valid means of assessing an important part of a clerk-typist job, whereas a graduate-level test of abstract thinking is likely to be irrelevant and hence invalid for that job. On the other hand, the abstract thinking test is more relevant than the typing test for graduate selection. An assessment method, in short, is valid or not valid with respect to a particular job or class of jobs.

Before using an assessment device its validity for the intended use should be researched and verified. Manuals for reputable tests and other commercially available methods provide reports on their validity. Validity may be ascertained in several ways, 'criterion-related validity' being widely considered to be the most convincing. A method has this kind of validity if it has been demonstrated in practice that people who score high on it also perform well on the job, and people who score low on it do poorly on the job. Criterion-related validity can also be tested against other indicators of organisational 'success' such as scores obtained in training.

The job-relevance of a method can also be established by demonstrating that its content is the same as, or very similar to,

Guidelines for choosing assessment methods

METHOD	Screening	Formal Qualification	Intellectual Effectiveness	Learning Aptitude	Job Skill Knowledge	Personal Qualities	Interpersonal Qualities	Career Development	Conduct
					PURPOSE				
Application form/curriculum vitae	++	+		+	+			+	
Reference checking	++	+++	+		+				++
Biodata	++								
Biographical interview	++	+		+		++	++	++	+
Personnel record	+				+				++
Record of qualifications	++	+++	+	+	+++				
Personal history & career interests				+		+		+++	
Performance appraisal	+++				++		+	++	
Technical interview		++			++				

Guidelines for choosing assessment methods

PURPOSE

METHOD	Screening	Formal Qualification	Intellectual Effectiveness	Learning Aptitude	Job Skill Knowledge	Personal Qualities	Interpersonal Qualities	Career Development	Conduct
Situational interview			+		+	+		+	
Knowledge test		Equiv	+		++			++	
Skill test	++				++				
Cognitive test	++		+++	+++				++	
Personality questionnaire				+		++	+	++	+
Assessment centre			++			+	++	+++	
In-depth psychological assessment			+++	++	+	+++	++	+	
Trainability test				+++			++		
Job performance test					++		+		
Group exercise			+			+	+++		

important parts of the job, as is the case with trainability and performance testing. This kind of validity, known as 'content validity', is clearly dependent on having done a sound job analysis.

A psychological test or other method that has been found to be valid for a job in one company can sometimes be assumed to be valid for the same or similar jobs in other companies. The idea that validity can be generalised in this manner is particularly useful for small organisations who have difficulty conducting their own validation research. Information about the applicability of a particular tool to other settings can usually be obtained from its designer, from the supplier or a consulting psychologist.

Credibility and acceptability

In practice, faith exerts a far greater influence than validity, most assessors being too readily persuaded about the value of an assessment tool because it looks or feels right. They make easy targets for unscrupulous or merely naive and ill-informed salespeople.

Nevertheless, how an assessment method appears to candidates is an important consideration particularly if it is being introduced for the first time. Methods that have the appearance of being related to the job, that is have 'face validity', are usually more credible and acceptable to candidates. Psychological instruments often do not look as though they have anything much to do with the job and, hence, lack immediate plausibility. Face validity gives no guarantee of any other kind of validity; instruments that are face valid may or may not be effective for selection.

Fairness

To reduce the chance of unfair biases in their selection practices, assessors should refer continually to the job analysis to ensure that what is being assessed is indeed a bona fide job requirement. Methods should also be scrutinised for questions or language that are sexist or racially biased. And the manager-assessor should regularly monitor the records of numbers hired, promoted and rejected for signs of bias. The question of fair discrimination is an important one that Chapter 11 explores in greater depth.

Cost effectiveness

A number of hard business questions must be posed when chosing or designing an assessment tool. What are the direct and indirect costs of designing a reliable and valid in-house method? What are the purchase costs? What are the costs of administering the method? Is it more economical to maintain a permanent staff or to use consultant psychologists and third-party contracting? Does it make sense to use external consultants to design the method and train internal resources to operate it? How do these costs compare with the potential costs of getting a selection decision wrong? In the worst case, how much will it cost to move out a person who has been wrongly selected?

Administration and scoring time

There is wide variation in the amount of time required for the administration and scoring of the various assessment methods. An assessment centre, for instance, may involve two administrators and several manager-assessors for anything up to three or four days, exclusive of training time. A situational interview for a single candidate might take an hour for a manager-assessor to administer and 20 minutes or more to score. A properly trained administrative member of staff might take an hour to administer a cognitive testing session for 15 to 20 candidates and complete the scoring in a further three to four hours.

In setting up the assessment plan it is critical that adequate time for administration and scoring should be budgeted.

Expertise

The pivotal issue in the success of the assessment programme is the quality of the staff or consultants who are to be involved. Whether they are selected by a formal or an informal process, the manager-assessor should be particularly careful. Capable people can be trained within a relatively short space of time to administer and score most of the methods listed on pages 46–47. Some of the more advanced personality instruments and in-depth psychological assessment which require a professional education and training in occupational psychology do not fall into that category.

For certain methods, most notably situational and technical interviews, assessment centres and trainability and performance tests, the assessors should be practicing and credible managers or supervisors who have or have had direct line supervision of the target job. Occasional exceptions to the rule are acceptable. For instance, occupational psychologists have been used successfully as assessors in assessment centres. A number of consultants, agencies and suppliers offer training although, as in most areas, it is up to the user to evaluate their credentials and ability to deliver.

Multiple measurement

Research has shown that a more reliable, rounded and useful understanding of a candidate may be gained from using several assessment methods and more than one assessor. This stands to reason since different methods measure different competences. This is one of the benefits of combining psychological tests and questionnaires into a test battery, or several complementary exercises into an assessment centre. This belt-and-braces approach also applies to the assessment of individual criteria. Each selection criterion or competence should be measured where possible by more than one method.

Organising the stages of selection

Stages can be thought of as a series of gates through which applicants must pass until they reach the final goal of appointment to the desired position. Only rarely are all candidates exposed to all stages of a selection process. It is more normal to eliminate a proportion of applicants at each stage until the successful applicant, or applicants, have been finally selected. The first example, shown opposite follows a fairly standard series of stages for entry-level hiring of train crew in Canadian National Railways. The other example shows the selection stages for the British Airways Senior Management programme described in Chapter 3.

How are the selection stages decided? How elaborate need the process be to give sound results efficiently?

Examples of selection stages in two assessment programmes

TRAIN CREW CANADIAN NATIONAL	SENIOR MANAGER POTENTIAL BRITISH AIRWAYS

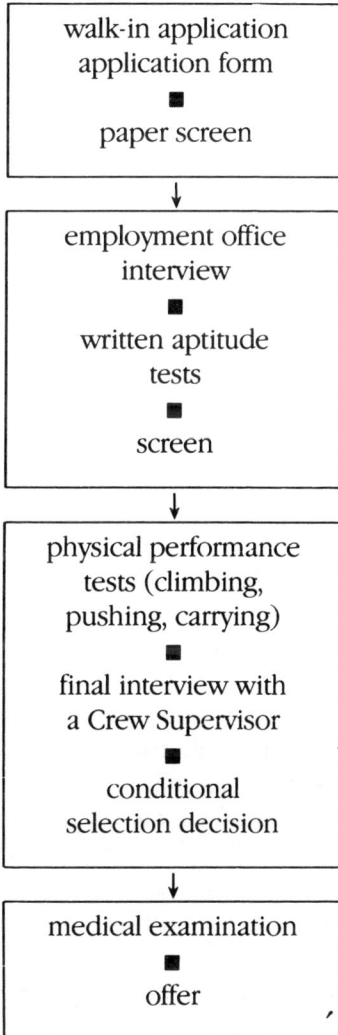

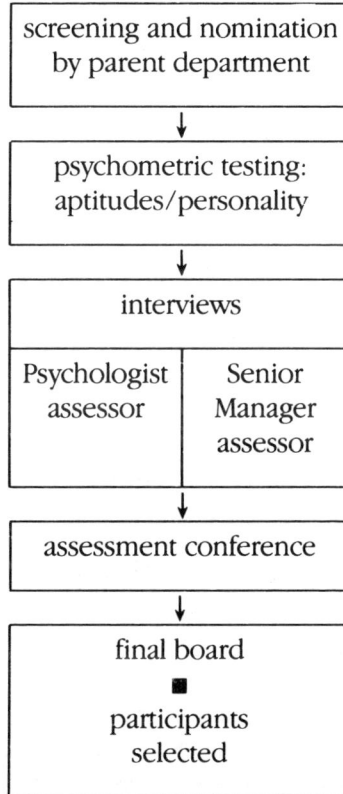

walk-in application
application form
■
paper screen

↓

employment office
interview
■
written aptitude
tests
■
screen

↓

physical performance
tests (climbing,
pushing, carrying)
■
final interview with
a Crew Supervisor
■
conditional
selection decision

↓

medical examination
■
offer

---

screening and nomination
by parent department

↓

psychometric testing:
aptitudes/personality

↓

interviews

Psychologist assessor	Senior Manager assessor

↓

assessment conference

↓

final board
■
participants
selected

Selection decision models

One of the first considerations is the most effective way to combine assessment data for the purpose of making selection decisions. A 'compensation approach' means that all the assessment methods are administered to all candidates, no one is rejected out of hand until all the stages have been completed. The results are combined and the candidates receiving the highest total scores are selected. In this model no single job competence has a critical status, strengths in one being seen as compensating for shortcomings in others.

A 'minimum competence' model is quite different: candidates must meet a prescribed standard of the competence or competences considered essential for the job. More often than not a 'mixed decision model' is applied: candidates must achieve minimum competence on key threshold requirements (for example trade qualification or programming experience of a specific kind) and are then rated on their total scores on other important competences. These might be assessment centre scores, or scores on a valid ability test.

In designing an assessment programme it is sensible to place at an early stage in the process the minimum competences which are simple to measure, and to defer the rated competences, which are difficult or costly to measure, to later stages .

Screening versus selecting

A clear distinction must be understood between screening and selection stages. Screening confirms basic qualifications that can be assessed objectively and used for short-listing candidates. For example, nationality, formal education, professional certification and craft qualifications, specific and verifiable work experience or achievements. Subsequent stages are for more extensive assessment to gain a deeper understanding of the short-listed candidates.

Inexperienced interviewers sometimes confuse screening and selection. In neglecting to investigate essential qualifications at the screening interview they may waste everyone's time with a fruitless and costly second interview. Conversely, in the second interview, the inexperienced manager may do little more than cover information already available in the candidate's application form.

Scale of the recruitment project

The number and nature of the selection stages will depend on the number of vacancies, the number of applications and the level and nature of the vacancies. When the applicant/vacancy ratio is very high the challenge is one of designing stages that whittle down the applicant numbers efficiently while at the same time discriminating effectively between those best and least suited for the post. At the other extreme, where the number of applicants virtually matches the number of places, the task may be simply to establish the individual candidates' minimum competence by means of a single-stage assessment. If the advertised vacancies are not all for the same job, then there may be greater need for a more elaborate assessment to find the best and most satisfying fit between the individual applicants and the available job slots.

To illustrate these points, a standard application form and a 30-minute interview might suffice when filling a vacant position for a mail-room clerk for which only a few applications have been received. On the other hand, hiring 50 or 60 graduate trainee accountants might involve processing three or four hundred replies to an advertisement, the same number of initial interviews, a subsequent visit by 150 or so of the applicants to the firm's main office for psychometric testing, an assessment centre for the top 100 and a final interview with a staff partner for the surviving 70.

Prospect of finding a suitable candidate

If a large proportion of people in an applicant pool are more or less equally capable and equally willing to do the job, and this can be established simply, then there is little point in designing an elaborate and expensive series of selection hurdles. The task is then simply one of deciding an equitable way for selecting among candidates who are equally suitable. If on the other hand relatively few people in the pool are suitable, then correspondingly greater effort is required to identify them.

53

Costs of the stages and the availability of staff

From a practical resourcing point of view compromise must always be struck between the ideal and the practical. Potential benefits of the selection stages must be weighed against their costs: materials and candidate travel, staff costs, and lost opportunity costs of assessors' time. Are there staff available to perform the administrative, screening and assessment tasks of a stage? Advance preparation to promote the advantages of the selection process is sometimes necessary when the cooperation of resource managers must be won.

Time available

The more stages there are the more time it takes to carry them out. Correspondence with and repeated visits by candidates are time-consuming. Advanced planning and detailed estimation of time involved are an essential part of organising the programme.

Planning and scheduling the assessment day

The schedule

In the interests of efficiency and economy it is advisable to organise as much of the assessment process as possible within a single visit and a single day. Manager-assessors and candidates who are currently employed can rarely spare more time than this and their needs must be respected. In designing an assessment day (or part of a day) appointments should be scheduled to minimise dead time for candidates and assessors. Sufficient time must be budgeted between exercises to allow assessors to review and consolidate their observation notes. It is recommended that comfortable rooms should be set aside, one for the assessors and one for the candidates. Advance arrangements should be made for beverages and lunch to avoid catering delays. Further suggestions for organising the physical facilities are made in subsequent chapters.

Assessment programme for Purchasing Manager candidates

08:00	Arrivals and greeting			
08:20	Briefing on schedule and order of the day			

CANDIDATES

	A	B	C	D
08:50	Ability testing for all			
10:30	Management interview	Technical interview	Psychological interview	Personality testing
12:15	Technical interview	Management interview	Personality testing	Psychological interview
14:00	L U N C H			
15:00	Psychological interview	Personality testing	Management interview	Technical interview
16:45	Personality testing	Psychological interview	Technical interview	Management interview
18:30	Farewell	Farewell	Farewell	Farewell
18:30	The Assessors' selection conference			
20:00				
20:00	Assessors' Departure			

In the sample assessment day outlined above the assessment methods consisted of: an interview with the director to explore the candidate's managerial abilities; a technical interview with a board of purchasing experts; and a psychological assessment based on

THE MANAGER AS AN ASSESSOR

aptitude testing, a personality questionnaire and an interview with a psychologist. The four candidates identified as A, B, C and D were tested as a group immediately after the greeting and briefing. Each of them then followed an individual schedule for the balance of the day. The programme culminated in a selection conference at which all the assessors shared and discussed their findings for each of the candidates and then made a selection decision.

5 Preparing for the interview

Key points

■ *The interview is the assessment method most widely used for making promotion and selection decisions. Its wide popularity is due to its versatility, ease of use and the opportunity it gives to 'sell' the job to the interviewee.*

■ *Different types of interview have different strengths and weaknesses, the semi-structured behaviourally-based approach is probably the one best suited to most manager-assessors.*

■ *The situational interview, a relative newcomer to the assessment scene, shows considerable promise.*

■ *Research shows that the selection interview does its job badly. It is generally unreliable and poor at predicting future performance and potential.*

■ *By organising and planning the interview in advance the accuracy of selection and promotion decisions is greatly improved.*

■ *It is important for interviewers to prepare: a structure to follow, competence dimensions that are clearly defined and targeted, and questions that will reveal relevant information.*

The versatile interview

The selection interview is one of the most venerable and established methods for promotion and selecting people into employment. Flexibility and adaptability of use are two of the main reasons for its great popularity and acceptance in the occupational world. Its advantages are many:

- it can be used for almost any type of job vacancy and candidate
- it can be used for gathering wide-ranging information about a candidate covering many different qualities, qualifications and personal circumstances
- it can be conducted in many different physical locations provided that certain minimum standards are met
- most people can learn to use it reasonably proficiently, it does not require a specialist to be administered effectively
- the interview provides a two-way flow of useful information between the parties involved
- a considerable amount of important information can be obtained in a relatively short space of time
- it appeals to managers because they can test for 'personal chemistry'. It gives them an opportunity to meet the potential addition to the team in the flesh
- the manager also has an opportunity to 'sell' the job and the organisation to the promising candidate.

Different types of interview

There are several different types of selection interview for the manager-assessor to consider.

The structured or patterned interview

In the structured interview, all questions and rules for scoring and interpreting them are pre-specified and strictly adhered to. There is no latitude to digress or follow interesting tangents, and control of the interview rests firmly in the hands of the interviewer. Structured formats are rather similar in concept to biodata forms and are usually designed for particular positions in a particular organisation.

The structured interview is good at eliciting factual information on a candidate's basic qualifications for the job. It can be carefully designed to avoid questions that violate equal employment or human rights. And it is well suited to interviewers who have little training, particularly those who interview infrequently.

A disadvantage is that it fails to provide candidates with an opportunity to communicate pertinent information that falls outside the rubric of the interview. Candidates may find its question-and-answer format off-putting and resent the impersonal aspect.

The unstructured interview

An unstructured interview is one where the questions, the order of the topics covered, the very topics themselves and the basis for evaluating them are not standardised in any way. The interviewer is free to take the discussion in any direction. In the hands of a highly skilled interviewer who knows his purpose and the job specifications, this form of interview can be highly effective. He is able to get the interviewee talking freely about himself, revealing things that a structured approach could never elicit. As most employment interviewers lack this level of skill and run the risk of losing control of a wholly unstructured interview, this approach is not usually recommended.

The semi-structured interview

The general approach that seems to suit most managers most of the time is the semi-structured interview. This combines flexibility with the security of knowing exactly what has to be covered during the course of the interview. Interviewers feel the semi-structured approach gives them control without alienating the interviewee or destroying the flow of the interview.

The situational interview

The situational interview is a relatively new and highly promising addition to the assessor's tool kit. In this very highly structured interaction, the interviewer presents the interviewee with a true-to-life situation drawn from the business or working environment. The interviewee is instructed to imagine himself in the target job and to give an oral account of what he would do in the situation. Apart from the occasional non-directive probing question, the interviewer does nothing but silently record what is being said. After several such situations have been presented and answered the interview is concluded and the answers are evaluated against predetermined assessment dimensions. The example below shows the kind of question that might be put to a candidate for a management position. An effective answer would require considerable shrewdness and practical intelligence as well as an understanding of how to manage inter-departmental relations.

This type of interview bears a similarity to traditional interviews in which the candidate is presented with practical scenarios to respond to. A notable difference is that greater effort is made in the situational interview to identify critical situations and to standardise them and the scoring to ensure equal treatment.

Practitioners can have confidence in the validity of this method as research has shown that what a person says he would do in a situational interview is generally what he actually does in practice.

Sample question for a situational interview

You are the Finance Director of Adzo Chemicals, a medium-sized industrial chemicals company. The industry is highly competitive and Adzo is competing with the large multinationals to retain its domestic market share. Several of the older-fashioned and less efficient companies in the business are facing closure.

At an executive board meeting to decide how best to handle the crisis, the Marketing Director is strongly advocating diversification into a wider product range to be able to compete on a broader front. Making his case with equal conviction, the Production Director is arguing for fewer not more products on the grounds that simplification of production would bring significant cost reductions. Faced with this impasse the Managing Director turns to you and asks which view you would support and why.

What would you reply?

The technical interview

For any job that requires prior work-related expertise or experience, the technical interview is an essential part of the selection process. Whether it is a separate interview or part of a more general all-purpose interview, its objectives are the same: to estimate the candidate's technical, professional or functional know-how, and to determine if it is sufficiently high to meet the standards of the organisation. A technical interview guide for a purchasing and supply management vacancy is p esented on pages 62–63.

The application form and the curriculum vitae are often the interviewer's starting point when exploring a candidate's technical competence. Questions focus on particular experiences and test the candidate's ability to apply specialist knowledge to practical situations—'When you were working on the development of the new inventory control system, how did you go about analysing the existing manual system?' The situational interview approach might also be useful to assess technical know-how.

A point to consider in the technical interview is just how much specialist expertise is actually required on the job, for there is sometimes a tendency to apply standards of craftsmanship or technical knowledge that exceed requirements.

The board interview

An approach that seems particularly favoured by central government departments in several countries is the board interview. This approach involves a single candidate and two or more interviewers who usually take turns at asking the questions. The Civil Service Selection Board in the UK is an example. Among its advantages, it offers several views of an applicant and it allows non-questioning members to focus their attention on watching and listening as a colleague deals with the task of marshalling and directing the questions. It is important that the interviewers should agree in advance their roles, the content areas each will cover and the timing of their questions. Without this degree of planning the Board can be a frustrating experience, as interviewers compete for centre stage, overlap their questions, or inadvertently interrupt one another and generally keep themselves and the candidate off balance.

One of the singular disadvantages of the board interview is that

A technical interview guide for a Purchasing and Supply Manager

POSITION: Purchasing and Supply Manager

TECHNICAL INTERVIEW

SCORING SHEET FOR:................DATE:.......
(Candidate's Name)

		Importance Weighting	Rating	Comment
1	Qualifications	2		
2	Relevant experience	2		
3	Career aspirations	3		
4	Understanding of company operations	2		
5	Relevant product knowledge	1		
6	Managing the P & S function	3		
7	Understanding role of P & S	3		
8	Strategic awareness	3		
9	Performance management	3		
10	Supplier analysis	2		

	Importance Weighting	Rating	Comment
11 Procedures & systems	2		
12 Techniques	2		
13 Negotiation skills	3		
14 People management	3		

Importance weighting
3 = highly critical   2 = important   1 = desirable

Candidate rating
1 = does not meet criterion   2 = just meets criterion
3 = meets criterion well   4 = meets criterion very well

it can be a decidedly stilted and threatening experience, particularly for external candidates unfamiliar with the practice.

Problems with interview preparation

The versatility of the interview and its ease of use are its weakness as well as its strength. It is used by managers in many different fashions, with widely varying standards and skill, and with variable consistency and effectiveness. The volumes of research published on the validity of the interview as a personnel selection tool have not been at all encouraging. If the truth be known, in untutored hands and even with a degree of training, it is not much better than chance in identifying the best candidates.

Apparently, no amount of evidence is likely to dissuade many thousands of managers from continuing to use the interview. In view of its strong following but low level of accuracy, improving interview practices must surely be considered one of the manager-assessor's priorities. The quality of external appointments and internal promotions depends on it.

THE MANAGER AS AN ASSESSOR

Absence of purpose and direction

Before starting their interview many poorly prepared interviewers are not clear about what purpose they are aiming to achieve in the next hour, or how they are going to proceed with it. During the interview this confusion of purpose and direction reveals itself in vaguely worded questions and rambling language which, at the end of the day, leave candidates confused and the interviewer not sure what sense to make of it all.

Interviews unsupported by any kind of pre-planned structure have several disadvantages:

■ the interviewers tend to talk too much and not listen enough
■ they give inconsistent results across interviewers, one thinking a candidate good whom another has judged poor
■ the unstructured approach is harder for the interviewer to control than an interview that is structured or even semi-structured
■ important areas of experience and ability are neglected and important evidence is overlooked or misinterpreted.

Poor definition or indeed the complete absence of job and person specifications is a major obstacle to the efficient gathering of relevant information. The forward planning and time management, which are necessary for analysing the job, its qualifications and its most important qualities, are all too often absent from the interview preparation.

Questions that miss the mark

If the wrong questions are put there is only a remote chance that the interviewee will give the right answers or the interview yield the right information. The task of the assessor, whether in an interview or an assessment centre, is complex and demanding. A great deal of attention, concentration and skill are required to listen, extract and take note of the pertinent remarks made by candidates. Furious thinking about what to ask next is obviously not going to help. There is no substitute for a list of thoughtfully prepared questions suited to the candidate and to the specific details of the job.

Bringing the same tired questions to every interview to put to every interviewee regardless of the nature of the job is simply not good enough. There is no such thing as a generic job or an all-purpose interview that suits every position and circumstance.

Expecting too much from the interview

Flexible and adaptable though it is, the interview is not a universal assessment tool. It cannot be all things to all managers for all assessment purposes. There are human qualities that the interview does not assess well but which are assessed efficiently and effectively by other means.

Some practitioners believe candidates' 'intellectual depth', or 'intellectual breadth' can be accurately estimated by their ability to answer some obscure question of rather less than general knowledge. Pet questions of this sort are a waste of valuable interview time.

Effective preparation that works

These difficulties are readily avoided by doing some preparatory homework. Putting one or more of the following points into practice should bring measurable improvement to the selection interview.

Be clear about the purpose

Normally, the chief purpose of the selection interview is to predict how effective a candidate's job performance would be if given the job. At the risk of stating the obvious, this can only be achieved by gathering reliable evidence about the candidate's ability, potential and motivation to meet the demands of the target job. Can this person do the job effectively and *willingly*?

The second purpose is to ascertain personal chemistry or 'fit'. Will the candidate fit in with the style of the hiring manager? Will he or she function as an effective and harmonious member of the team and be willing to align his or her values to those of the organisation?

Throughout the meeting with the candidate the interviewer should remain continually aware of the job that is to be filled, its organisational context, and the people with whom it is mainly concerned and at the same time continually dig for signs of matching qualities in the candidate.

Defining what to look for

The steps to follow mirror the job analysis process described in Chapter 2:

- if the organisation has carried out analyses of this kind before, then these will provide illustrations, or possibly generic position profiles, as a starting point
- identify the main responsibilities and the most important outputs of the job
- define the qualities and qualifications that are the most critical to successful job performance
- determine which of these key requirements can be suitably assessed by means of an interview—define them and write out the 'interview dimensions' and the statement of qualifications in full
- if possible, develop positive and negative indicators to 'anchor' each dimension as illustrated in the example opposite which looks at the candidate's ability to give direction
- the results of the analysis are the cornerstones of the assessment interview.

Designing an interview structure

There is a wealth of structured interview formats to help keep the interviewer on track. Some are organised around the dimensions and criteria of interest, others detail the planned sequence of steps and topics the interviewer intends to cover. In the example for the position of purchasing and supply manager (pages 62–63) the assessment topics are in fact listed in the order that they were investigated in the interview. For this position a total interview score was computed for a candidate by multiplying the 'candidate rating' score by the 'importance weighting' for each topic, then summing these products. This kind of scoring procedure greatly enhances the objectivity and reliability of the interview.

An example of a dimension-referenced interview at the end of the chapter covers eight primary dimensions with allowance for

Positive and negative indicators for 'direction'

DIRECTION: the ability to generate strategies, plans and tactics based on a sound assessment of priorities, facts, risks and possibilities.

POOR		ACCEPTABLE		EXCELLENT
1	2	3	4	5

Positive indicators

- develops business strategies that are challenging and sound
- sets priorities based on corporate direction and a good assessment of the facts, risks and possibilities
- sets logical action plans anticipating and making provision for contingencies
- controls and adapts plan to events as they unfold
- communicates the direction credibly to all affected oriented visions

Negative indicators

- strategies and plans are non-existent or unrealistic
- ideas are narrow and limited to events and beliefs of the past
- concentrates attention and resources on the wrong issues
- no contingency planning, unquestioningly accepts the givens, no 'what if' thinking
- fails to communicate direction, loses support

further supportive evidence relating to additional strengths and weaknesses. Under each of the dimensions are listed a few exemplary behaviours which would be taken as positive evidence for that dimension in the applicant. Space is provided for recording the essence of the interviewer's observations on the applicant

THE MANAGER AS AN ASSESSOR

together with a 5-point rating scale for evaluating the applicant on the dimension.

The trouble with using a format like this as a literal guide is that the course of an interview rarely follows the sequence in which the dimensions appear on the page. People are too complex to be neatly packaged in this way. To take an obvious example, oral skills cannot be linked to a specific episode in the interview but are present or missing throughout the exchange with the interviewer. Similarly an applicant's responses are likely to display positive or negative signs of 'balanced judgement' at various points and not just in response to a specific question.

The real advantage of a framework based on dimensions comes not so much during the interview as beforehand and afterwards. A careful preview and rehearsal of the eight key points fixes in the mind the behaviours on which attention should be concentrated. When the interview is over this format is ideal for summarising and rating the observations made during the interview. This format does *not* dictate the sequence of the interview, but it is a useful reference guide and worksheet for writing up the results after the interview is over.

The kind of structure that is useful not only before but, more importantly, during the interview is a schedule of the things to do and in what order to do them. A 20-point plan shown in Chapter 6 helps the interviewer cover the interview agenda. In planning the interview it may help the reader when using a schedule like this to allocate real times to the main steps. Keeping close to these times is an obvious way to improve weak time management.

The reader can take comfort in the research findings which show that interviewers who follow a systematic structure are considerably more consistent in their judgements, and much less likely to overlook important job requirements, than those who do not.

Preparing questions that focus on the assessment dimensions

Preparation for the interview should include questions devised to 'get at' the assessment dimensions. Generally speaking, these should be open-ended and directed at the 'what', 'how', 'why' and 'when' of the candidate's real experiences. The well-prepared interviewer might even wish to map out some tentative 'probing' questions as follow-up to the open questions. For illustrative purposes, a sample set of questions designed to explore the candidate's abilities on the dimension of 'direction' is set out below. In examining these examples the reader might also consider the potential of questions about who was involved in an experience and how they were involved. These are invaluable for revealing important people and relationship issues in an applicant's work history.

Questioning on 'direction'

Open-ended   'Would you take a few minutes to tell me about the business goals and objectives you have (were) set for the current year.'

Narrowing   'What were your priorities and how have you gone about managing them?'

'Where are they now?'

'What were the major steps in your plan to implement the new information system?'

'Where has the project reached?'

Probe   'Why has the project become stuck?'

'I don't quite understand how your subordinates were reacting during the implementation phase. Could you take me through that part again?'

'Why?'

While the course of the interview will differ from one case to another, by adhering fairly closely to a common line of questioning a high level of consistency and comparability across candidates can be achieved.

Many prepared questions will elicit pertinent evidence on more than one dimension, and indeed designing 'multiple-dimension questions' makes for an efficient interview. As some questions may not fit some candidates, it is useful to prepare some back-up questions.

Trialling the interview

To improve the reliability of the interview, design it and then try it out with volunteers or role players before going live. Two assessors should interview the same 'candidates', make their judgements independently of one another, then compare and discuss them in detail afterwards. Through this process of comparing views, exploring differences of perception and interpretation, and by adjusting their ways of evaluating a candidate's responses the interviewers will develop shared standards and a high degree of interrater reliability. In practice it is very rare to see this level of commitment and it would be desirable to see more of this kind of practical training-cum-research being done.

Now that everything has been planned and prepared, how does it work on the day?

Non-technical interview dimensions for purchasing and supply manager

POSITION: Purchasing and Supply Manager

NON-TECHNICAL INTERVIEW

SCORING SHEET FOR: . . . . DATE: . . . .
(Candidate's Name)

1 **Self projection**

■ dress and grooming create favourable impression
■ engages in discussion in a relaxed, open manner
■ controls own emotions to respond in a calm, objective and constructive manner

HIGH   5   4   3   2   1   LOW

EXPLANATION:

2   **Oral communication and presentation**

■ expresses ideas in a clear and informative way, avoids vague or ambiguous statements
■ communicates specialist information in language readily understood by the layman

HIGH   5   4   3   2   1   LOW

EXPLANATION:

3 **Initiative**

■ seeks out and takes responsibility for all that happens
■ independently identifies needs, priorities and goals
■ originates, precipitates action to achieve goals and results

HIGH   5   4   3   2   1   LOW

EXPLANATION:

4 **Achievement motivation**

■ sets high standards of performance, sets challenging and realistic goals
■ strives to do things better, to improve the operation, reduce costs and time factors, and to improve quality

71

HIGH	5	4	3	2	1	LOW

EXPLANATION:

5 Balanced judgement

- considers and weighs relevant issues, conditions and alternatives before committing himself
- views situation objectively and reasonably free of personal bias

HIGH	5	4	3	2	1	LOW

EXPLANATION:

6 Analysing and solving problems

- keeps his or her antennae out, identifies problems; seeks out the relevant information, relating data from different sources; identifies possible problem causes
- identifies and extracts the essentials from complex information
- generates workable and efficient solutions

HIGH	5	4	3	2	1	LOW

EXPLANATION:

7 Planning and organising

- identifies necessary strategies and actions, in sensible

sequence and timescales, for self and others to accomplish objectives and targets

HIGH   5   4   3   2   1   LOW

EXPLANATION:

8 Controlling

- understands how and wants to build checkpoints for monitoring progress and evaluating plans and actions
- wants to measure the function's and his own performance and identifies measurable indicators

HIGH   5   4   3   2   1   LOW

EXPLANATION:

9 Other observed strengths

10 Other observed weaknesses

11 Overall interview rating

HIGH   5   4   3   2   1   LOW

EXPLANATION:

6 Making the interview work on the day

Key points

- *The most common interviewing pitfalls include: a physical set-up that is unfriendly to candidates, poor time management, letting the interviewee take control of the interview, closed and leading questions, excessive friendliness and unnecessary stress, psychological speculation.*
- *Frequent interviewer biases include: stereotyping, 'halo and horns' effects, 'just-like-me' biases, 'contrast' effects, the 'central tendency' and personal liking for a candidate.*
- *Good interviewing practices include: candidate care, a candidate-friendly setting, maintaining control and some distance, encouraging the candidate to open up through appropriate questioning, concentrating on performance and behaviour.*
- *Personality has a strong influence on the behaviour of both the interviewer and the interviewee.*

This chapter moves on from the preparation to look at the conduct of the interview itself. Interviewers need to know something about the different types of interview that can be used advantageously in the selection process. The chief types are described in the last pages of the chapter.

Failings on the day

The wrong scene

Some of the most common shortcomings are timing and physical factors that disadvantage the interview candidate:

- poor time management—keeping the candidate waiting beyond the time scheduled, cancelling the interview without notice, and running out of time
- seating the candidate at a level below the interviewer, so that looking at the interviewer is awkward
- visual glare from natural or artificial light sources making it difficult for the candidate to see the interviewer's face and causing discomfort
- a large table or desk acting as a barrier between candidate and interviewer
- a noisy environment, distracting external noise, telephone calls and other interruptions.

Quite apart from the inconvenience and physical discomfort they cause, these habits convey a general lack of caring. Whether or not this is the intended message it is the one that candidates will take away and use for making their own selection decisions.

Getting out of control

With the best of intentions an interviewer can easily lose control of the interview, because he rambles on, or because the clever or voluble interviewee takes charge and steers the interview along a path of his own choosing. The session overruns, the interviewer does not achieve his objectives and the accumulating delays mean the last candidates have to be rescheduled for a later date.

If you are talking you can't be listening

In the traditional unstructured interview, as noted earlier, the interviewer generally does most of the talking. Untrained interviewers with no clear brief to follow talk for more than half the time. This is not a problem if he has made up his mind to offer the job and the main object of the interview is to give the interviewee information or to convince him to accept an offer. But it is a major problem if the interviewer has yet to make up his mind and is still gathering information. Trained interviewers working to a clear plan are estimated to talk about 20 to 25 per cent of the time.

Questionable questions

The aim of the good investigative interviewer is to get the subject to do most of the talking. To accomplish this he must pose the right questions and phrase them the in the right way. The form in which questions are put can defeat this purpose. Closed questions, like 'Do you like working with people?', 'How many years have you been employed?' invite single-word replies. The longer this kind of questioning goes on the shorter the candidate's answers become and the more the interview declines into an interrogation. Leading questions should only be used sparingly and selectively to confirm an item of fact such as, 'When did you leave school?'

The unsubtle interviewer also telegraphs what he or she is looking for with words like 'I don't suppose . . .', 'I expect . . .', 'Presumably . . .' Most candidates are astute enough to work out the most desirable answer and respond in a way that is socially desirable. On the other hand, the candidate may avoid elaborating or qualifying an answer to such a question so as not to appear to disagree with the interviewer.

No follow through

Another shortcoming is to accept at face value a candidate's claim to qualifications or competence in a particular area. Because the critical follow-up questions go unasked, undeserved claims to formal qualifications or work achievements may go undetected. Sometimes this is due to the interviewing manager's blind faith in human nature; often it is because of an unwillingness to probe deeply.

Being too nice

The aspiring talk-show host should beware. This is the interviewer who treats the interview as a friendly chat with someone he hopes

will be as agreeable and as interesting as himself. He might satisfy
his social and affiliative needs but little else. Erring in this way the
interviewer is not going to feel comfortable about asking the difficult question or following up on the uncomfortable issue that the
applicant would rather see ignored.

Unnecessary stress

At the opposite pole is the stress interviewer who mistakes a candidate's tolerance of bad manners with the capacity to function
under pressure. They are not the same thing. Stress interviews have
the double disadvantage of alienating suitable candidates. Again,
this is not to say that the interviewer should side-step sensitive
areas, or that he must not pursue a tough line of questioning with
vigour and determination. But it does mean that gratuitous stress,
like gratuitous violence, probably does more harm than good and
ought not to have a place in the normal selection interview.

Fishing in deep waters

Some managers and personnel officers are tempted to play ama-
teur psychiatrist in the selection interview. Over-interpreting body
language is one of the potential risks. Body posture and hand ges-
tures usually have more to do with everyday itches and simple
habit than unconscious conflicts.

Drawing conclusions about the candidate's values and motivations from his account of early childhood relationships is also very
risky. Asking him to describe himself in three words, a favourite
gambit of some interviewers, is quite misleading. It takes years of
professional training to be successful at this approach and the
sensible manager would do well to stay with more tangible and
verifiable information.

Typical interviewer errors

Beginning with the pioneering studies of psychologists at McGill
University in Canada much has been learned about the influence
of the interviewer on the process and the outcome of the interview. Every interviewer's personal biases and beliefs affect his

judgement and, hence, the outcome of the interview. 'Observer errors' are found in all forms of assessment involving live interaction between the observer and the observed. In the main they are:

The similar-to-me error. Interviewees with similar backgrounds, attitudes and perceived personality to the interviewer are rated more favourably than those who are seen to be different.

The sequence effect. The interviewer's evaluation of an applicant is affected by the impression left by the preceding candidates. This 'contrast effect' works for or against the individual depending on the strength or weakness of the preceding candidate.

Stereotyping. Interviewers carry around in their heads a personal concept of an 'ideal' or 'good' candidate. They tend to compare candidates against this stereotype whatever the job and the specified competences.

The predominance of negative evidence. Unfavourable evidence carries more weight than favourable in the evaluation of a candidate. Interviewers tend to look for reasons to reject; a candidate is more usually selected because no reason has been found for rejection than for positive strengths shown. Interviewers are often disinclined to take a chance on a candidate who has any manifest weakness.

The primacy effect. A first impression is formed early in the unstructured interview, usually in the first four minutes or less. The interviewer then tends to focus the questioning to find evidence to confirm it.

The halo effect. A candidate who receives positive evaluations on one or more of the interview dimensions will tend to be given higher evaluations than he or she deserves on all the dimensions; the converse of this, the 'horns effect', is equally true.

Central tendency. This is the error of the cautious or unsure interviewer, the tendency to avoid errors in judgement by rating everyone in the middle of the scale—evaluating everyone as average.

Personal appearance. A tendency to draw inferences about a candidate's qualities or characteristics from purely physical appearance, for example, all red-headed persons are impulsive, men with beards and sandals are unreliable. The height of a candidate tends to influence interviewers' judgements, tall men being viewed as more capable and intelligent than short men.

Personal liking. Interviewers are usually not emotionally detached, they give significantly higher ratings to applicants whom they personally like.

The contrast error. The tendency of interviewers to rate candidates as opposite to themselves on a trait. For example, an extremely orderly interviewer may see anyone who does not match his standards as disorderly or careless.

The leniency error. Some interviewers are easy raters, others are tough.

Equating enthusiasm with competence. Inexperienced interviewers commonly confuse interest and likes with competence. Just because a candidate is keen about marketing does not necessarily mean the experience or the potential to be an effective marketer is there. Enthusiastic expressions of willingness to undertake a job may be no more than wishful thinking. The interviewer must investigate if the level of ability accords with the expressed motivation.

How to be a successful interviewer

Setting the right scene

In setting up the selection interview, the interviewer should keep in mind the impression he or she wishes to convey to interviewees when organising the reception area and the layout of the interview room. Selling the job and the organisation to candidates is an important part of it.

The following points may appear so transparent they do not need to be said, but in practice they are all too often absent:

■ make sure that someone is detailed to receive the candidates, know their name and who they are to meet, offer tea, coffee or a soft drink and provide comfortable waiting space
■ remove any barriers in the interview room; seat the interviewee at right angles to the interviewer to encourage more open discussion and disclosure; use an occasional table and comfortable chairs of equal height; consider placing an ashtray for the candidate's convenience unless the interviewer has a medical reason to avoid secondary smoke
■ ensure the room is temperate and free from noise disturbance

79

with comfortable room lighting; position the chairs to avoid backlighting from windows
- position the manager's chair to provide an unobtrusive view of a clock or watch
- staff should be advised to ensure there are no interruptions directly or by telephone.

Taking control and keeping it

The interviewer should:
- start with a printed outline of the interview structure, including the main questions he intends to ask
- keep track of what has been learned and what has still to be uncovered by taking brief notes
- deal with one point at a time and not allow himself to be deflected from the point. If the interviewer does decide to follow a tangent, then he or she should make a brief note and come back to the main point as soon as convenient
- keep the evasive candidate on topic, and ask probing questions until satisfied. Red herrings should be recognised as diversions from sensitive topics that ought to be explored
- set the pace of the interview by using appropriate questioning. It is important to pick one's time, interrupt an over talkative interviewee and move the interview on to the next topic or question
- stay away from areas that are irrelevant to the main purpose, no matter how interesting they might be.

The outline that follows will act as an aide-memoire for the selection interview. By establishing in advance the approximate time to devote to each step the interviewer will be able to manage and control the interview more efficiently.

Questioning and listening

What kinds of things do skillful interviewers actually do to help people open up?

They put the interviewee at his ease, show acceptance and understanding and display interest in him as an individual and

A 20-point plan for the selection interview

Before the interview:

1 Review candidate's paperwork:
   - curriculum vitae or resume
   - application form
   - summary report from previous interview

2 Identify particular areas to explore.

3 Have the key assessment criteria clear in your mind.

4 Have the prepared positive and negative indicators clear in your mind, but remember they are only indicators.

5 Review the prepared open-ended and follow-up questions.

6 Candidate care: arrange for the candidate to be greeted, for beverage to be on offer and for payment of travel expenses if this is company policy.

7 Set the scene: arrange clock, lay-out, seating, lighting of interview room; divert potential interruptions.

At the start of the interview:

8 Greet candidate by name, putting him at ease with appropriate small talk.

9 Seat him comfortably, inviting him to smoke if he wants.

10 Reduce his uncertainty by outlining the content of the interview and when it will conclude. Explain the stages and timing of the overall selection process.

During the interview:

11 Start questioning on a subject easy for the interviewee to talk about, keep more sensitive items until later.

12 Establish his career aspirations and what he expects from the job under consideration.

13 Put any queries you may have (about qualifications, job

history or education) from the screening interview, application form or curriculum vitae.

14 Move into the prepared dimension-based questions.

15 Make sure you are taking notes.

16 Review your notes to ensure you have covered all the dimensions.

17 Invite his questions, describe the job, the conditions and the organisation.

18 Tell him the interview is concluded, listen carefully to what he says now it is 'off the record'.

19 Thank him for being open and helpful in coming to the interview. Ensure that he is accompanied to the exit from the building and knows where to get his transportation.

After the interview:

20 **Immediately** review and analyse your notes and recollections, evaluate the interviewee on each of the dimensions and prepare the paperwork for a selection conference, if there is one.

---

what he has to say. They tune in to the candidate's asides, inviting further elaboration. These asides are often revealing.

They ask the right type of open and probing questions, adjusting these to suit the candidate.

They respond with comments that restate and reflect what the interviewee says. Restatement, or rephrasing in one's own words, is a way of showing an interest in understanding the interviewee's experience and views. It is a very effective way of encouraging a two-way communication flow. Reflecting is similar, but what is reflected is the feeling rather than the content of the interviewee's words—'You seem to be a little uncomfortable discussing that incident'. These approaches help to overcome defensiveness and reticence; they are also a check to ensure that the interviewer has correctly understood what the candidate has said.

A skilled interviewer may apply subtle pressure to encourage the interviewee to talk by means of pauses and silences. Pausing after a question is effective; it indicates to the interviewee that he is expected to contribute. The inexperienced interviewer loses some of the advantage by rushing into a pause to clarify a question that is already clear.

Effective interviewers take whatever time is required to do all of the above well. Unrealistic time pressures and demands to 'process' more interviewees than is reasonable in the time available are at cross purposes with these questioning and listening techniques.

Maintaining the right distance

The selection interview is not about befriending or bullying candidates; it is about gathering hard information in an objective and professional way to help make a risky and often expensive investment decision.

While it is important to treat the interviewee with respect and consideration, the attitude of the effective interviewer is one of objectivity rather than sympathy. It is important to conduct a thorough and searching examination that will lead to a confident and business-like selection decision. Graduate recruiters have found that companies with rigorous assessment processes are likely to win candidates' respect. Candidates want to feel they have had ample opportunity to demonstrate their strengths and potential.

Concentrating on behaviour and performance

Experts in human psychology strongly advocate that selection interviewers should concentrate on behaviour, what the interviewee says and what he says he has done. Certainly it will continue to be necessary to draw inferences about the motivations, intentions and values of the interviewee; evidence of this kind is essential if sound decisions are to be made. But these inferences should be drawn from hard behavioural evidence not some fuzzy fabrication about the candidate's 'inner person'.

The example at the end of Chapter 5 illustrates the point. Instead of dealing with rather vague and ambiguous terms like 'maturity' and 'intellectual breadth' this interview is about behaviour and behaviour that has quite specific meanings. Certainly it still leaves considerable play for the interviewer's values and judgement but it comes closer to objectivity than interviews that purportedly explore the candidate's psyche.

Personality and interviewing

The interplay of personalities in the interview deserves some further comment. As mentioned earlier, perceived similarity and liking are two aspects of the interviewer's personality that exercise a significant influence on his interview ratings and selection decisions.

Research has shown that the personality of the interviewer also plays a significant part in graduates' decisions to accept an offer of employment. In fact this personality factor is sometimes more influential in this decision than salary, the conditions of work, or the nature of the work itself. The attraction function of the interview in recruitment is not to be underestimated, particularly in times of competition for scarce manpower resources.

7 Objective testing in personnel selection

Key points

- *Psychological tests assess either capacity (aptitudes, abilities, skills, knowledge) or habitual behaviour (personality, values and interests). Both kinds are usually efficient and economic to use, but they must be administered, scored and interpreted by trained personnel.*

- *Objective ability tests which assess general intellectual functioning and more specific abilities are the ones most widely used for personnel selection. Common tests of special abilities include verbal, numerical, spatial and abstract thinking and critical reasoning.*

- *Some achievement tests are useful for assessing skills like reading, grammar and spelling, clerical coding and checking, typing, word processing and various operator skills. Others assess the ability to apply a body of professional or technical knowledge to realistic tasks and problems such as book-keeping and accounting.*

- *Performance tests, or standardised work sample tests are used to assess a person's ability to perform critical job tasks. The test experience gives candidates a taste of the job. Trainability tests have been developed mostly for craft jobs.*

- *Self-descriptive personality questionnaires are easy and economical to administer and score, but are more complex to interpret because of the complex interactions that take place between the individual and the job environment. They should be used in combination with observed behaviour.*

Psychological testing has a long-established history as a method that is reliable, valid, efficient and cost-effective. Despite compelling research evidence showing it to be one of the best predictors of future job performance, this method of assessment has found a surprisingly limited market in the businesses of the UK, particularly in small businesses. The objective of this and the next chapter is to demystify testing and give the manager-assessor a flavour of how tests might be put to advantageous use.

What are psychological tests?

Psychological tests are systematic procedures for measuring abilities, skills, personality traits and other ways in which individuals are psychologically different. It will be convenient here to broaden the definition to include also tests of knowledge and physical ability. Most are paper-and-pencil devices but a few require candidates to use or operate a physical instrument or piece of equipment such as a typewriter. Tests are particularly appropriate for assessing non-behavioural aspects of individuals, such as original thinking, spatial reasoning and aggressiveness, that are difficult or time-consuming to evaluate in other ways.

The two types of tests most frequently used for personnel selection are commonly known as 'maximum performance tests' and 'habitual performance tests'. Maximum performance tests:

- have right and wrong answers
- measure an individual's ability or achievement under competitive conditions when he is doing his best
- place demands on the test-taker's capacity by requiring him to work against the clock or by the intrinsic difficulty of the items
- usually allow individual test-takers to be ranked from strongest to weakest on the function being tested.

Habitual performance tests:

- are self-descriptive questionnaires that focus on personality characteristics, interests or values
- provide indications of a person's most typical behaviour, his

preferred way of behaving, his feelings about himself, or interpersonal relationships.

The main types of tests

There are several thousand commercial tests available to managers directly or through an occupational psychologist. To do more than briefly describe a small sample is clearly beyond the scope of these chapters.

General ability tests*

Tests of underlying mental abilities have a very good track record for predicting future performance and are used to assess general mental functioning and learning aptitude for many different jobs and occupations. Tests of general mental ability usually comprise verbal and numerical problems, often include abstract thinking problems as well and yield an overall score.

Selecting a test that is at the right level of difficulty for the intended test-takers is important. If the test is either too easy or too difficult then it will not be discriminating since everyone will achieve around the same score. The AH series of tests (1), which is very widely used in the UK, is graduated by level of difficulty: the AH4 and its parallel forms, the AH3 and AH2, are suitable for the general population; the AH5 and the AH6 for above-average candidates such as university graduates and middle-senior managers. Similarly, the Raven Progressive Matrices test (1), consisting entirely of non-verbal items, is available in standard and advanced versions for the general population and for those whose roles or occupations demand a high level of reasoning ability.

Other ability tests

Selection tests of primary mental abilities or aptitudes cover verbal ability, numerical reasoning, spatial ability, mechanical reasoning and critical thinking. Mechanical reasoning tests, like the Bennet Mechanical Comprehension Test (12) and the ACER Mechanical Reasoning Test (1), are frequently used for trade and craft jobs and for apprenticeship selection. As tests of this kind usually entail a

* *See* Appendix 5 on page 175 for names and addresses of test suppliers coded by a number in parenthesis in the main text.

knowledge of simple mechanics and therefore measure achievement as much as ability, care must be taken to ensure they do not discriminate unfairly against female candidates who are less likely to have pursued a science curriculum at school.

The Graduate and Managerial Assessment (1) tests of verbal, numerical and abstract thinking are interesting and challenging instruments designed for the very capable candidate. The numerical and verbal tests have high face validity for business and could well be found to be content valid for specific applications. There is a user group and the test supplier is able to provide appropriate industrial norms.

The Watson-Glaser Test of Critical Thinking Ability (12), which

---

A sample item from the Watson-Glaser Test

DIRECTIONS

For the purposes of the test assume that everything in the paragraph below is true. The problem is to judge whether or not each of the proposed conclusions follows beyond a reasonable doubt.

Paragraph

In a large town where the drink-driving laws are rigidly enforced, it was found that only 30 per cent of drivers breath-tested were completely alcohol-free during a certain period. Among those who were married, however, 50 per cent were completely alcohol-free during the same period.

Proposed conclusions

1 Strict enforcement of the drink-driving laws did not prevent 70 per cent of drivers drinking sometime during this period.
2 If drivers had to be married, their drink-driving record would improve.
3 Less than 30 per cent of those drivers who were unmarried were completely alcohol-free during this period.

---

has been available for many years, has become a model for other more recent tests and remains a useful and widely used test. It is an objective multiple-choice test of the ability to think logically and objectively and to work through complex verbal arguments. One of its advantages is that it can be used for people with average to high levels of intelligence. A minor drawback for some test-takers was the American wording of the items, but this has now been rectified in a new version appropriate to British customs and culture.

Sample items from railway recruitment tests

Reading skill

'Hand signals (using flags and lamps) are used to control train movement. Signals must be given from a point where they can be plainly seen and in such a manner that they cannot be misunderstood. If there is doubt as to the meaning of a signal, or for whom it is intended, it must be regarded as a stop signal.'

From his locomotive cab an engineman sees a green light. He does not know if the signal is meant for him or not. What must he do?

☐ 1 Move the train forward.

☐ 2 Slow the train down.

☐ 3 Stop the train.

☐ 4 Back the train up.

Spelling skill

Words that are spelled correctly

		word1 only	word2 only	both words	neither word
1 tariff	shedule	☐	☐	☐	☐
2 capacity	clearance	☐	☐	☐	☐

Numerical reasoning ability

At 09:45 Train 625 leaves Confederation Station for St. Pierre 50 miles away. It travels for 20 miles at 80 miles per hour and is then held up for seven minutes by repair work on the track. Because of poor track conditions the train continues for the next 10 miles at 30 miles an hour. It then resumes its normal speed of 80 miles per hour. At what time will Train 625 arrive at St. Pierre?

- ☐ 1 10:04
- ☐ 2 10:28
- ☐ 3 10:42
- ☐ 4 10:51

Occupational abilities

A number of tests of special abilities have been devised for particular jobs or special applications, such as programming, computer operations, word processing and foreign language learning. Clerical aptitude tests fall into this category though they might also be thought of as skill tests. One of the most interesting recent developments in this field has been the Berger series of aptitude tests (9) for programming (B-Apt), computer operations (B-Coat) and word processing (B-Word Aptitude). Based as they are on thorough job analysis these tests are similar to trainability tests and have a very high degree of content and criterion validity. One disadvantage is that they are administered individually and are expensive when compared with other perhaps less predictive tests.

Many tests of perceptual-motor abilities have been devised to measure hand-eye coordination, finger dexterity and manual dexterity which are obviously important in jobs involving the use of tools and the monitoring or operation of machines. These tests are used most often as aptitude measures for selection into training and apprenticeship schemes. In an very comprehensive assessment programme for selecting cadet pilots, British Airways used a sophisticated computer-driven set of tests to assess eye-hand-foot coordination and instrument-reading ability. At the other end of the sophistication spectrum a candidate for a craft apprenticeship might have the task of transferring ball-bearings from one box to another with tweezers as a test of his finger dexterity.

Skills and knowledge tests

Skill tests fall into two broad, often overlapping, categories: basic skills like reading, arithmetic and oral communication; and specific job-related skills such as clerical skills and operator skills. Clerical tests are designed to assess a person's skill and speed in checking the acuracy of verbal and numerical material, coding and filing information, spelling and grammar, and word meaning. Developers of clerical skill tests like the Modern Occupational Skills Test (1) and the Automated Office Battery (10) design them as a package of complementary instruments that may be used as a battery or separately as the user chooses.

Operator skills tests, such as tests of typing, instrument reading, word processing and programmer coding proficiency, are undoubtedly useful but, since they are usually administered individually, are less economical than group tests.

Objective multiple-choice tests of job knowledge are occupation-specific and expensive to develop. Developing a knowledge test really only makes economic sense for repeated applications with large numbers of candidates, or where possession of the job knowledge in question is critical to performance. For other situations the manager might consider the less expensive option of designing a suitable situational interview to assess job knowledge.

It should be noted that a professionally designed knowledge test does not stop at measuring recall of facts and principles but calls into play the ability to apply the knowledge in solving a job-relevant task or problem. Used as part of a qualifying examination or as an equivalence test, testing objective knowledge is one of the best ways of evaluating an important part of professional competence.

Achievement tests of skills and knowledge are intended to assess the degree to which a person has profited from his or her learning experience, whether through formal classroom learning or practice in the work place. Provided the content sampled in the test is a valid representation of what is required in the job then it is likely to be a good predictor of future performance.

Job performance tests

The closer a knowledge test comes to sampling the content or simulating a job the more it is a work sample test. Work sample tests fall into two broad classes: those that assess an individual's current ability to perform a job, or a crucial part of it, such as a Heavy Goods Vehicle driving test, and those that assess the ability to learn and perform the job effectively in the future. In either case the design starts with a very detailed observation of a skilled performer, an analysis of what he or she does and how, and a determination of a performance standard. Job performance and trainability tests must be designed to be highly standardised, performed by all applicants on comparable equipment, and have a reliable scoring guide. In certain situations it is possible to administer the test on real machinery or work equipment. For instance, a job candidate in a women's hairdressing salon might be required to bring her own model and style her hair as a sample of her work. In others, for reasons of safety or cost, it must be done in a simulation as when using a flight simulator for pilot assessment and selection.

Performance tests have been developed for many craft and technical jobs and to assess physical as well as psychological abilities. Physical performance tests designed to assess the abilities of lifting, carrying and pulling are fairer and more valid than arbitrary minimum height standards which discriminate against women applicants and many racial minority candidates.

Indeed research has shown that performance tests generally have high criterion and content validity. They provide test-takers with an opportunity to preview the job and to make a more informed choice if offered the job. In the UK, the Industrial Training and Research Unit (5) has devised a number of valid trainability tests for craft jobs such as lathe operating and carpentry, and for other quite different occupations like dentists and helicopter observers.

The disadvantages are that job performance tests generally have narrow applicability to a specific job or occupation, they may become outmoded when the job content or the technology of the job changes and they may require the use of costly equipment.

Habitual performance questionnaires

Every reader of the Sunday newspaper supplements is already familiar with personality quizzes. Their frequency of appearance is a measure of how much people are interested in knowing more about themselves and how they compare with others. Personality inventories and values questionnaires are very similar in appearance, but each one is backed by an infinitely greater body of psychometric research and design work. Properly developed questionnaires are able to give much more reliable and valid descriptions of a person's personality, temperament, interests and values.

They generally consist of self-descriptive statements, like, 'I find it easy to strike up conversations with strangers', to which the test-taker indicates concurrence or otherwise by ticking a true-false or a yes-no option. Each statement is one of a number which, when marked in the keyed direction and added up, give the test-taker a score on a 'trait' or a 'preference'. Scales of traits and preferences are 'bi-polar' in that opposite ends of the scale have opposite meanings (for example, introvert-extrovert, dominant-submissive, impulsive-restrained). Sample bi-polar dimensions appear at the end of this chapter, on page 97.

By comparing the individual test-taker's scores with a 'norm table' of scores obtained from a group of similar individuals, his or her relative standing on each trait or preference can be learned. This procedure is described on page 99 of Chapter 8. An examination of the pattern of scores would lead to provisional inferences about the individual, for example—compared with other middle managers in the XYZ company, Mr. J appears to be moderately introverted, submissive in the extreme, but with a very high need to exercise control over things and people. The process of understanding Mr. J does not stop here: the ideas emerging in the interpretation of the questionnaire should either be explored in an interview or cross-checked and supplemented with other assessment information.

Among the many personality questionnaires that have been successfully developed for use with normal populations and have shown promise in personnel selection are: the Guilford-Zimmerman Temperament Survey (0), the Gordon Personal Profile Inventory (11), the Myers-Briggs Type Inventory (7), the 16 PF (1), the California Personality Inventory (7), and the Occupational

Personality Questionnaire (10). A new entrant on the market that shows promise is the Managerial and Professional Profiler (6) which has high reported reliability and a large number of job-relevant scales including several interesting-looking values dimensions.

The complexity of personality

While personality and values questionnaires are economical to use, scored objectively and efficient to administer and mark, they are rather less reliable and valid than mental ability tests. In many of the research studies published on this topic no evidence of criterion validity has been found for many personality questionnaires and scales. One difficulty is that personality questionnaires often pose questions that have no apparent relationship to the world of jobs and occupations and, hence, have little face validity. And, being heavily influenced by the cultural context in which they were developed, their suitability for assessing people from other cultures is often questionable.

Personality measurement is of course a highly complex area and we do know that several factors complicate the relationship between an individual's degree of success in the job and his scores on a personality questionnaire. Typical work behaviour, first of all, is not shaped just by a person's preferences and traits but also by the particular circumstances, the particular job and the ways in which these factors interact with his personality. The circumstances he happens to find himself in at the time, as well as his more enduring personality, will also influence how he answers the questions in a questionnaire. Under conditions of organisational stress, for instance, his scores on certain scales may change. Finally, as a characteristic that is desirable in one occupation or organisational culture may not be desirable in another, it is impossible to generalise about which dimensions to include in a selection decision.

Another factor that reduces the efficacy of personality questionnaires in selection is the tendency to inflate one's positive qualities, particularly when there is a desirable job at stake. To get around this, the statements making up most though not all personality questionnaires have been worded or structured to neutralise the effects of such response tendencies.

Even when these various caveats are taken into account, personality questionnaires can add much to the assessment process and to a deeper understanding of individual applicants. Their practical value can be enhanced by the following provisions:

■ doing a thorough analysis of the job and its environment will give clues to the aspects of personality that are most critical
■ the person interpreting the scores must be trained on the instrument and experienced in its use—an area where the manager-assessor will find the services of the supplier and an occupational psychologist useful
■ the questionnaire should be used in conjunction with a searching interview or an assessment centre.

With suitable training non-psychologists may be authorised to use some of these instruments but clearly great care must be exercised in their interpretation.

A note of caution

Caution must be exercised when interpreting an individual's scores on ability tests, particularly a single score on a general test. Although the intention behind general ability testing is to assess capacity and aptitude, not achievement *per se*, it has been found immensely difficult to remove from test items the effects of experience, not just educational experience but exposure to reading material generally. Since intelligence can only develop and grow through the individual interacting with his environment, this is hardly surprising or in any way damaging to the legitimacy of the tests. But it does mean that less well educated people may not show themselves up to best advantage. Therefore, while undoubtedly useful and predictive of success, ability scores should not be taken as the be-all and end-all of selection for several reasons:

■ there is more to intellectual competence on the shop floor or in the board room than can be measured by standard paper-and-pencil ability tests
■ there are usually other required competences, equal to or greater in importance than tested intellectual ability, that should not be forgotten in the selection process

■ no method of assessment is foolproof; there will be occasions when capable applicants score badly, due perhaps to excessive anxiety, lack of exposure to books and general reading material during the formative years, or because they come from a different culture.

Typical bi-polar dimensions of personality

CAUTIOUSNESS

Impulsive, acts on spur of the moment, makes hurried or snap decisions, enjoys taking chances, seeks excitement.

Highly cautious, does not like to take chances or run risks, considers matters very carefully before making decision.

ENERGY LEVEL

Much physical activity, strong drive; highly productive, rarely becomes fatigued.

Slow and deliberate in action; prefers a slow pace, low productivity.

ORIGINAL THINKING

Likes to work on difficult or complicated problems; curious, enjoys thought-provoking questions and discussions; likes to think about new ideas.

Dislikes working on difficult problems; does not care to learn; no interest in thought-provoking issues, prefers routine problems.

---

8 Using psychological tests

Key points

- *The advantages of using psychological tests include: standardisation, equality of treatment, objective scoring, administrative efficiency, relatively high reliability and validity, and the provision for comparing candidates.*
- *Ability and other maximum performance tests may be used on their own to screen and short-list, or in combination with other assessment data for other management uses.*
- *There is no single best way to set passing scores that is universally accepted in all circumstances. Several ways are described, some based on population norms and others based on expert judgement or the results of validity research. Some of the disadvantages of setting passing scores are discussed.*
- *Communication and candidate care are particularly important when introducing and operating a new assessment system—and especially when psychological testing is involved.*

Continuing in the aim of making psychological tests and questionnaires more accessible to the manager, this chapter describes the main things to look out for when choosing objective tests and introducing them into an organisation.

The advantages

The same for everyone

The same questions or problems are presented to everyone in exactly the same way and under the same time limits. Standardisation promotes fair treatment and means the test-takers can be compared meaningfully with one another on the specified assessment dimentions.

Objective

Test-takers' responses are marked according to predetermined rules, there is nothing subjective about it. Objective pass-fail standards can be set with greater assurance than other more subjective methods that depend on assessors' judgements.

Efficient

Paper-and-pencil tests are designed to be administered in the format of multiple-choice questions, brief written answers or longer essays. Multiple-choice formats are the most common, they have greatest objectivity, speed of administration and scoring, and several candidates can be assessed at the same time. It is believed that a wider range of functions can be reliably assessed in a given space of time with the multiple-choice format than with any other form of assessment. Scoring normally takes just a few minutes with a simple template. Written response formats are much more difficult and time-consuming to score, require subjective judgement and are less reliable. Other types of objective testing are rather less efficient to administer because they involve the physical operation or manipulation of a machine, objects or a piece of equipment.

Comparison with 'test norms'

The test manual supplied with a test or questionnaire includes 'test norms' which have been developed by administering the instrument to a large number of people then grouping their scores into bands, from high to low, in a table. This is known as standardising the test. By referring a job applicant's test score to the table the test user can establish the applicant's standing relative to that norm group. Frequently, there will be several norm tables for different 'populations' of test-takers.

Tables of test norms are usually expressed in terms of 'percentiles': for example, the test score that was exceeded by 50 per cent of the standardisation sample is known as the 50th percentile, the score exceeded by 20 per cent of the sample as the 80th percentile, and the score exceeded by 75 per cent of the sample as the 25th percentile. Using a norm table a candidate's test score can also be placed in a percentile range as in the following hypothetical example:

Test score	Percentile Range
21–23	top 5%
18–20	next 10%
16–17	next 20%
12–15	mid 30%
8–11	next 20%
5–7	next 10%
0–4	bottom 5%

Reliable and valid

Developers of reputable psychological instruments have established their reliability and validity by carrying out research studies in commercial or public service settings. Detailed information should be reported in the manual, including the types of occupations or jobs for which a test has been found to be valid.

The main uses of tests

Psychological testing may serve a variety of purposes in an organisation.

Screening and short-listing

One of the perennial questions faced by managers in the selection process, particularly when the ratio of candidates to vacancies is high, is how to reduce the numbers to a manageable proportion. If, after using the application form to screen out applicants on essential job-related criteria, the applicant numbers remain unmanageable, there are two sensible options. One is to eliminate candidates randomly, perhaps on the basis of the order of receiving the applications. This practice is not universally acceptable and has brought a vociferous protest against certain London boroughs who have applied it. The other more publicly defensible way is to administer a group test or tests of maximum performance, that is job-relevant, and use the scores to short-list for the next stage.

In following this second course management is saying effectively that, everything being equal, it would prefer to have people with more rather than less of the ability in question. While this seems a perfectly reasonable business decision and one that is equitable, many applicants expect to have an opportunity to show their paces in interview and, hence, may take exception to this form of screening. However, provided the matter is handled sensitively and communicated in advance, the benefits of using tests to screen outweigh this potential disadvantage.

In combination with other methods

Tests may be viewed as an integral part of the whole assessment of the person, as pieces that contribute to the whole jigsaw. They might be used, for example, to generate hypotheses to explore in a subsequent interview. Or they may provide complementary evidence that sheds light on a competence assessed in some other way.

The assessors' challenge often is to tease out the likely reasons for any inconsistencies in performance and arrive at a reasoned judgement about the candidate's true ability or personality disposition. A candidate might perform well on a psychological test of critical thinking but do poorly on logical reasoning in a situational interview. Alternatively, he or she might do well in the situational interview and badly on the test. Weighing and evaluating psychological results in this manner requires experience and judgement but gives a more rounded and balanced account of the applicant's true strengths and limitations.

A test, or parts of a test, might also contribute to a total assessment score derived from all the methods used in the programme. Candidates could then be compared and ranked on their total weighted scores. Expert advice should be sought on the surest ways to determine the best weightings and combination of scores.

Alternative to educational qualifications

Aptitude tests may become highly valued as the means of establishing learning aptitude and general intellectual ability in preference to educational level. As employers continue to extend their trawl for competent people in non-traditional pools they will find that aptitude and ability tests may take the place of educational qualifications.

Personal development

One of the most promising trends is the growing use of assessment information to enrich individual candidates' insights into their own capacity, potential and development needs. Receiving feedback about the test results in a career counselling session allows the candidate to derive benefit from the selection process. Certainly for in-company candidates it is sensible to have personal development as an intrinsic part of the selection process.

Placement

Batteries of psychological tests and questionnaires, generating a profile of scores for each test-taker, can play a valuable role in matching individuals to jobs, fitting square pegs to square holes and helping management to make optimum use of their available resources. When the selection ratio of applicants to vacancies is very low and the most effective assignments of individuals to vacancies must be found, this use of tests to 'place' applicants is particularly helpful.

Team mix and team building

Questionnaires like the Myers-Briggs Type Indicator and Belbin's team role inventory provide revealing clues of the ways a person interrelates with others, his preferred roles in group situations and his preferred work environments. With feedback from instruments like these the members of an established team or a work group can better understand each others' strengths and blind spots and so learn to work together more effectively. Likewise for a manager in the privileged position of assembling a team from scratch, instruments like these may be a powerful aid to ensure a productive and harmonious mix.

Other organisational objectives

Psychological tests are a useful tool for the chief executive who has inherited a management group in a takeover or merger, particularly if performance appraisal records are meagre and incumbents are unknown quantities. Provided that it is handled sensitively, an assessment programme including psychological tests can be an invaluable source of information for deployment, development, promotion and outplacement decisions.

The application of knowledge testing in the workplace that is described on page 103 illustrates the potential this method has for improving the quality of work performance. A practical application of trainability testing in a sensitive industrial relations situation is described on page 104.

Setting passing marks

Though many different answers have been proposed possibly the thorniest question for the test user is how to set a pass mark. The most widely used methods are:

■ Setting a fixed pass-fail mark based on test norms. An organisation might have a quality control policy of short-listing

Using a technical knowledge test for quality control

Failure to recruit capable technical and professional staff at the junior level of a function has a negative impact on current efficiency and productivity, but it also affects the longer-term capability of the workforce. Too many incompetent staff at the junior level blocks the flow of talented people into and through the ranks.

This was happening in the financial administration function of the Public Service of Canada. It was decided that all applicants who lacked a professional qualification in accounting or financial management should be tested on their technical knowledge as part of the qualifying process.

A new objective test was designed based on a thorough analysis of accounting, budgeting and reporting practices in central government. The test items were designed to be equally fair to candidates from the private and the public sectors. Once the new test was implemented the intended improvements in the quality of financial administration soon followed.

The test consisted of 50 multiple-choice questions, took three hours for candidates to complete and was scored by computer. A sample question:

A company had a beginning inventory of $12,000 worth of product X. The cost of product X sold during the year amounted to $36,000 and purchases during the year totalled $40,800. The inventory turnover rate is (to the nearest one-tenth):

☐ 1 3.7

☐ 2 3.0

☐ 3 2.5

☐ 4 none of these

A revolution on the Isle of Dogs

The newspaper industry experienced the biggest technical revolution in its history with the change from hot metal printing to the new printing technology. In planning a relocation of printing plant and equipment to a new site at the Island of Dogs in London, the *Financial Times* made plans also for selecting and training staff on the new methods. The critical question was who among the existing staff should be retrained?

To assess individual learning capability, an analyst from the Industrial Training and Research Unit closely observed the new methods of operation in an existing printing plant, analysed the key steps and defined the performance standards. The five key tasks that were identified and described were the foundation for the design of a trainability test. The selection of the most able staff for re-training was entirely successful.

Just as important, this practical form of testing also proved to be very acceptable to the staff, no small achievement in one of the decade's worst industrial relations scenes.

Based on an original report which appeared in the *News Review* of the Industrial Training and Research Unit, November 1987.

---

only those candidates who achieve the 30th percentile or better on a general ability test.

■ Ranking the candidates in order, from highest to lowest, based on their normed scores and setting the passing score according to supply and demand.

■ For a knowledge or skill test, using the judgement of job experts to set a 'minimum competence' score. Anyone who gets at least a minimum competence score is, in the informed opinion of the job experts, sufficiently proficient in job knowledge (or skill) to perform the job. For jobs that have a high health or safety risk, as in a nuclear power plant, a high minimum competency score would be set.

■ Using the statistical techniques known as regression analysis to set a score on a test, or a composite of weighted scores from several assessment methods, as the passing point. This can only be done in the context of a criterion-related validation study which compares the test scores of a large number of job-holders with ratings of their performance or with some other measure of their effectiveness in training or on the job. The object of this method is to reduce the rate of rejection for capable applicants and to increase the rejection rate for applicants who are less capable of doing the job.

The problems with setting a hard-and-fast passing point, whatever the method, are:

- some worthwhile candidates will be rejected in error for the simple reason that no assessment tool is perfectly valid
- the candidate who has a bad cold or a headache or who has forgotten his reading glasses, the one from an ethnic minority background, another from another part of the English-speaking world . . . and similar practical issues encountered by test administrators
- people tend to resent being turned down by an impersonal non-interactive process in which they were unequal partners
- not enough candidates might reach the passing point thus creating a dilemma for the manager, whether to maintain the set standard or to drop it in favour of filling the positions.

In finding his way through this minefield of issues, the manager is advised to research the pros and cons of these various approaches and to seek technical advice for his or her own particular purposes and circumstances. If a normative approach is used it is advisable to develop in-company norm tables on known groups of people such as existing job-holders or applicants.

Getting started

Expert advice

Managers who want to take full advantage of psychological tests but are unfamiliar with testing would be well advised to take expert

Checklist for selecting a psychological test

1 Do you have sufficient grounds for believing that the test is measuring an important requirement for the job for which you intend to use it? Is it clear from a job analysis or a validation study you conducted or from information about validity generalisation?

2 Does it come with a manual that gives technical information and detailed administration instructions?

3 Is there more than one parallel form of the test in case you have to administer it a second time, or if one form should become compromised?

4 Is there an objective scoring key?

5 Is each of the scales measured statistically reliable? (Using conventional statistical measures of correlation, ability/aptitude tests should have test-retest reliability of .75 or better, habitual performance tests .65 or better.)

6 Does it have evidence of validity for the type of job and population for which you intend to use it?

7 Does it have norms for the type of job and population for which you intend to use it?

8 Do you have someone adequately trained to administer and score it and to interpret the scores?

advice from an independent occupational psychologist who has no commercial interest in the supply of psychological tests. The British Psychological Society maintains a register of chartered occupational psychologists. A chartered psychologist is able to advise and expand on all of the topics covered in this and the previous chapter. Some independent consultancies are listed in the appendices.

Suppliers and training

Properly developed tests are only available to people who are properly trained in their use. There are numerous suppliers of psychological tests, some of whom are also listed in the appendices, and many support their psychological tests with public and in-company training courses. General introductory courses lasting for one day are frequently offered for people exploring testing for the first time. There are slightly longer courses on general test administration, and courses lasting up to five days on the administration, scoring and interpretation of more sophisticated and specific personality tests.

Test batteries

When contemplating which tests would give the best value within the constraints of time and resources, managers will probably find themselves faced with a dilemma. Sould they select or design a specific test that gives precise and highly reliable measurements of a limited but important portion of the job requirements? Or should they use a number of tests that are less precise and individually less predictive, but which provide a broader and more comprehensive coverage of required competences? In recruiting graduate programmers, for instance, do they choose a precise instrument for assessing programming aptitude or do they use a broad-based battery of more general abilities?

Clearly there is no simple answer that applies to all possible jobs or in all circumstances. Nonetheless trends in the 1990s seem to favour the broad-bladed sabre over the narrow-pointed rapier:

- the pace of change in technology and in the job itself often requires the ability to adapt and relearn and a flexibility of style more than specific skills or specialised knowledge
- people are progressing to higher-level and less technical jobs relatively quickly
- given the supply shortage, placement and not selection may become the major use for psychological testing
- at the manual worker level, greater flexibility and transferability of skills are now at a premium to suit single status conditions and team working methods

- at managerial levels, similarly, building teams, keeping up with and steering change of all kinds, managing innovation and adjusting quickly to unexpected events are at least as important as specific functional knowledge in the mosaic of required competences.

For these reasons the manager would be advised to give serious consideration to using batteries of tests, though different batteries for different categories of job. To cover the abilities, skills and personal qualities deemed to be important to the organisation and the job the manager might choose to 'bundle' several hitherto unrelated tests and questionnaires. Or, alternatively, it may be sufficient to use an extant test battery like the Differential Aptitude Test (7) which covers a broad range of abilities: verbal, numerical, abstract reasoning, clerical speed and accuracy, mechanical reasoning, space relations, spelling and language usage.

Core assessment plus modular assessment

An issue that was raised in Chapter 2 bears some elaboration here: to select a unique set of tests and questionnaires suited to every individual job or, alternatively, to ignore job analysis and put every applicant, regardless of status or position, through the same sheep dip of tests. The first solution is almost never practical and the second is largely ineffective.

A tactic that works well is to have the same core battery (or assessment programme) for all the jobs in a given class, say the company's supervisors, while topping this up with a test or a questionnaire or some other assessment tool suited to the *particular* sub-class of supervisors. This would mean doing a job analysis on all the different types of supervisory jobs in the company to define the core requirements and the unique requirements. In the supervisor example, a core battery of psychological tests might be complemented by a special knowledge test or a situational interview or a performance test for administrative supervisors, production supervisors and maintenance supervisors. This is a practical solution that makes for considerable efficiencies in operating the assessment system, developing test norms and validating the tests.

In-company trialling and validation

Once a test or a test battery has been purchased the user should make every effort to trial it in-company with existing job-holders. A consulting psychologist will be able to design a validation and normative study for your organisation. Introduce testing gradually, retaining the scores for in-house norms but not using the results to make selection decisions until people in the organisation have developed a degree of experience and comfort.

Communication

Even where there is little respect for the traditional ways, people tend to view change with unease and distrust, particularly if it affects their job opportunities and careers. The introduction of newfangled tests, therefore, may well give rise to suspicion within the work force. Some, particularly those who have distant and jaundiced memories of school, will also find them daunting and bearing no obvious connection with the realities of jobs or work.

Information sessions and information booklets are needed to clarify misunderstandings, describe the tests broadly, promote the benefits of fairness and objectivity and give tips on preparation and test-taking. Post-test feedback and counselling should be offered and supplied by someone who is capable of delivering this important and sensitive service.

Candidate care

Assessing candidates in a caring way, and treating them generally with dignity and consideration, is a sound business practice as well as a humanitarian value. Assessment is a two way process after all. Candidates are forming opinions and drawing conclusions about the likely attraction, or lack thereof, of working for this interviewer, this department, this organisation. How candidates are treated at the recruitment stages has a great deal to do with their motivation to join and to stay with the organisation.

Test administration and scoring

It is imperative that testing is not carried out in just any old space that happens to be free or by any junior clerk who happens to have nothing better to do that day. A quiet, well-illuminated and ventilated room, complete with properly spaced tables and chairs, should be arranged in advance and a properly trained administrator should always be in control. No interruptions are permissible otherwise the test results are invalidated.

Computer administration and scoring

Facilities for administering and automatically scoring and norming several tests and questionnaires by personal computer are now available. A number too can be batched for optical scanning and scoring. Computer-generated text reports from personality questionnaires are potentially useful, though they do not match the richness of interpretation offered by experienced and expert test-users. Most test suppliers offer computerised facilities and software.

Security and access

Locked storage facilities supported by company policies governing security and access are a must for any test-user. Access must be strictly limited to those who genuinely need to know test results. Automated storage of results means of course that candidates have rights of access to the information under the provisions of the Data Protection Act.

9 Assessment and development centres

Key points

■ *The assessment centre method is used for selection, promotion and career development purposes. It is a particularly effective low-risk method for uncovering hidden potential.*

■ *The main features of the assessment centre method: being standardised it is fair to candidates; it simulates the critical aspects of the target job; each assessee is evaluated on multiple methods and by several assessors; the assessors are experienced line managers who understand the job; assessors are carefully selected and trained; and results feedback is given.*

■ *Several types of exercise commonly used in centres are described: group and individual tasks, written and participative tasks. Different tasks lend themselves to different competences.*

■ *The main steps for developing an assessment centre are: job analysis, identifying appropriate types of exercise, linking the exercises to dimensions, designing the exercises and scoring materials, standard setting, trialling, training and implementation.*

An assessment centre is a carefully designed programme of job simulations in which candidates' performance is observed and evaluated by several job experts who have been specially trained in observation and assessment. A development centre is very similar in design and structure but quite different in purpose. Assessment

111

centres are used to support selection and promotion decisions, and typically involve the participant in relatively little interaction with the assessor. The object of development centres is to enable participants to learn more about themselves, consequently the process engages them in much more feedback discussion with assessors. Some centres attempt to meet both objectives with variable success.

Many organisations in the public and private sectors of several countries use assessment centres for selection and promotion into management, supervisory, graduate and other positions. Its modern use in the UK has interesting origins. In 1941, the War Office Selection Board (WOSB) was struggling with the task of identifying a stock of suitable officer material but finding that the results of its formal interview approach were falling far short of requirements. As it happened a former military attache to Berlin, recently returned to Britain, was privy to the simulation-based approach used for officer selection by the German military. Thanks to his contribution WOSB was able to borrow and extend the idea of using simulation exercises and psychological assessment for the identification of leadership potential in their officer candidates. Subsequent validation research on the WOSB assessment centres established a respectable level of predictive value and this experience has continued to influence the thinking of British assessment practitioners.

However, the major influence on contemporary knowledge and practice has come to this country from the private sector in the United States. Indeed, much of today's orthodox wisdom about the assessment centre method and its standard practices can be traced to seminal research done at the American Telephone and Telegraph company in the 1950s and 1960s.

Characteristics of assessment centres

Simulating the job

The competence dimensions that are assessed in a centre are drawn from an analysis of the target job. The simulations are designed to represent critical tasks and aspects of this job, and to elicit job-relevant behaviours from candidates.

Programme administration

Instructions, exercise materials and procedures are all standardised and administered impartially to ensure a level playing field for all participants. The programme is organised and run by a trained administrator and usually lasts from one to three days, though some are designed to run longer. A typical centre caters for six to eight candidates with a candidate/assessor ratio of two or three to one. The programme is carefully planned to allow the assessors time to mark up their assessments after each of the simulation exercises.

Experienced assessors

Each candidate is assessed and evaluated by not one but several assessors in different exercises. Assessors are almost always line managers or supervisors with direct supervisory experience for the target position. Psychologists have also been used successfully as assessors, notably in the early American Telephone and Telegraph centres. Selecting and training the assessors are crucial to the credibility and success of an assessment centre. The example on page 114 illustrates the selection criteria applied by the Greater Manchester Police in the selection of assessors for the Force's promotion assessment centres.

The assessment process

This follows a logical sequence:

- during an observation exercise the assessor carefully observes the assessee's behaviour and takes notes; in a written exercise the assessee simply proceeds with the assignment.
- upon completion of the exercise the assessor summarises his or her observations, classifying and evaluating them under the prescribed competence dimensions. He or she may also assign performance ratings.
- at the end of the centre the assessors typically review and discuss each assessee's performance, integrating or pooling their

---

Criteria for the selection of assessors for the Greater Manchester Police Promotion Assessment Centres

- Is respected as competent operational officer and has supervised officers at the rank of the centre in an operational role.
- Has a reputation as an objective and fair appraiser of subordinates' performance.
- Communication skills are of a high order—able to listen attentively, use the spoken word to communicate thoughts effectively, and express observations and reasoning in a clear written form.
- Has integrity, placing a high value on confidentiality and honesty.
- Makes measured judgements, objectively balancing the various facts and circumstances before reaching a conclusion.
- Sound critical reasoning, identifies the assumptions, facts and logic of an argument and its relevance to an issue.

Reprinted from the *Police Review*, 9 March 1990

---

conclusions across exercises and reaching an overall assessment. Usually an overall assessment rating is assigned to each assessee.

The feedback process

When the assessees' development is the main objective of a centre, opportunities for feedback and discussion are incorporated in the design of the centre. When the objective is selection or promotion it is more difficult since interactive feedback would undoubtedly affect the dynamics of the individual assessee's motivation and behaviour. For this reason feedback is normally deferred until the assessment is over. Feedback of results and the career development counselling that flows therefrom is a critically important part of the assessment centre, regardless of its purpose, and should not be seen merely as an optional add-on.

Identification of potential

Assessment centres are one of the most effective methods for identifying potential especially with assessees whose job experience is widely different from the requirements of the target job. They also give job candidates a unique insight into the key aspects of the job. When an organisation wants to identify potential supervisors from among its operating or clerical staff the assessment centre method is difficult to beat. By being placed in a realistic but safe simulation of the working environment workers can demonstrate their aptitude and make mistakes without risk to the operation or safety and without jeopardising industrial relations. One of the great rewards in this application of assessment centres is the uncovering of unsuspected talents.

Fairness

A considerable body of research in the United States has shown that this method is extremely fair to candidates regardless of their sex or racial background and has been accepted as such by the courts.

Some typical assessment centre exercises

Leaderless group discussion

Six or so candidates are given a problem to solve and instructed to arrive at a group decision within a specified time limit, usually 30 to 40 minutes. While no leadership role is assigned, various other roles of equivalent status might be. The complexity of the assigned task, which can range from a simple topic such as a disciplinary case to a highly abstract value-laden topic, is matched to the demands of the target job. The group exercise is useful for assessing: social impact, group ascendance, oral communication, influencing skills, group process skills, persuasiveness, competitiveness, cooperation, empathy and relationship building. Because it is a good ice-breaker this is often chosen as the leading exercise of the centre.

Rotating leadership group

This is a somewhat more structured and formal group exercise. Again the group has one or more tasks to complete but in this group the leader role is assigned and then rotates as the exercise progresses. It is good for assessing the ability to lead others, gain commitment, and manage and control a meeting.

Business game group

Candidates in the group receive information simulating a business or other organisational environment. Under assigned or assumed roles they are required to plan and make a series of decisions about the fictitious business or organisation. This type of exercise is similar to management development games and is good at eliciting team working behaviour, the abilities to relate and communicate under pressure and business acumen.

Role-playing interview

The individual candidate is presented with a problem or an inter-personal issue and required to play the role of interviewer with a fictitious customer, supplier or employee. The interviewee role might be played by an actor, a manager or an employee. The briefing and training of the role-player is very important, otherwise the variability of his performance will defeat the requirement for consistency.

This exercise is useful for eliciting evidence on: oral communication, sensitivity, empathy, information gathering, problem analysis, supervisory style.

Fact-finding exercise

The candidate receives a description of the circumstances surrounding a problem or incident or a requirement for information and is then required to seek additional information from a resource person and make a decision within a specified time limit. All responsibility for structuring and timing the enquiry rests with the assessee. After the allotted time the assessee makes a brief oral presentation of his or her findings or decision. The exercise is used to assess the qualities of reasoning, information gathering, persuasiveness and ability to think and talk under pressure.

Presentation

The candidate is given a topic and 20 to 30 minutes to prepare a presentation. He or she then makes a stand-up presentation to the assessor acting the role of Managing Director, or to the participant group as the Board. This is sometimes followed by a question and answer session with the assessor. This is a useful exercise for assessing oral communication and presentation, and how well the candidate can represent the organisation in public or to a senior body.

Information-based presentation

This differs from the straight presentation in that the assessee is required to sift and analyse diverse information and prepare and deliver a stand-up presentation. Given data may be numerical, financial, text, tabular, or charts, depending on the information-processing demands of the target job. The task is to sort this information into some logical order, sort the irrelevant from the important, and cross-reference related information. A written report or a stand-up presentation may be prescribed as the means of presenting the solution. Good for eliciting indications of: working under pressure, managing large quantities of unfamiliar information, analysis, numeracy, financial or budgetary know-how, future-oriented thinking, presenting the information clearly, understanding of technical information.

In-tray exercise

Also known as an 'in-basket' test, this exercise simulates administrative tasks of a manager's job. Required to stand in for a fictitious job-holder the assessee's task is to go through the absent manager's in-tray which consists of carefully designed (often real) memos, letters, reports, desk diary and background information. He or she has then to read, evaluate, prioritise and 'action' these by arranging meetings, and by writing notes, memos, letters, or an analysis with recommendations, or an account of what he would do and why. Usually there is an urgency and time pressure imposed on the assessee. Good for assessing: prioritising, planning, organising and controlling; efficiency and effectiveness under pressure; information handling and analysis; decision making; delegating; clarity of communication; personality characteristics related to style of dealing with people.

Designing an assessment centre

Customised assessment centres are often developed for in-company use, but in addition exercises and complete centres may be purchased off-the-shelf from suppliers. Some of the main points to consider when designing an in-company centre are outlined below.

Key players

The involvement of the job 'owners' or supervisors and the designers is essential. The tasks of the job supervisors are:

- to provide the content of the job at the analysis stage
- to provide real-life incidents as the kernels of the exercises
- possibly to draft the exercises and the scoring materials
- to set and agree performance standards
- to participate in the trialling of the centre as assessors and evaluators
- to act as assessors when the centre goes live
- to provide feedback to the participants.

The role of the assessment centre designer is:

- to structure and manage the processes for job analysis and defining the competence dimensions
- to advise on the types, strengths and suitability of exercises for different levels of participant, and their sequence in the centre
- to design and edit exercises, scoring materials, operating procedures and assessors' manuals
- to train the job experts on design and the assessors in their role
- to design a feedback process and train the feedback givers

■ to ensure that the centre fits within the organisation's system and policies for managing the human resource.

Dimension and exercise matrix

Once the job analysis is completed and the key dimensions of competence have been identified and clearly defined (see Chapter 2), the next step is to select exercises and tests that will elicit behavioural evidence of those competences. This requires both judgement and experience of what types of exercise are best suited to both the competences and the level of the prospective participants.

Quite naturally, the number of competences that can be assessed depends on the duration of the centre and the richness of the exercises. However, it is important to keep in mind that assessors do not have unlimited capacity to observe and process behavioural information. Accordingly, it is prudent to avoid the risk of exceeding their capacity by linking only a few dimensions to a given exercise. On the other hand, as illustrated opposite, each competence should be linked to enough exercises in the design of the centre to ensure that the candidate is assessed on it at least twice. A useful rule of thumb is to limit the number of competence dimensions in a centre to around eight to ten.

A scoring and reporting system

Customised observation sheets for recording the assessees' behaviour should be prepared. Also required are marking guides and scoring sheets that reflect how observed behaviour should be categorised and rated for each dimension. A manual should be designed for the assessors with a detailed explanation of how to use these documents.

Two opposing views are held about the degree of structure that should be built into the scoring system of a centre. One view is that comprehensive definitions of the competence dimensions and the scoring guides impose blinkers on the assessor preventing him from observing relevant and important behaviours. According to the opposing position, well-defined scales, checklists, behavioural statements indicating positive and negative behaviours and structured marking guides greatly increase the reliability of ratings and ease the burden on the assessors.

Linking dimensions and exercises

This matrix shows which exercises will be used to assess the dimensions of a fictitious assessment centre.

ASSESSMENT
DIMENSIONS   ASSESSMENT EXERCISES

	BI	SI	IT	GD	Test	PQ
Oral communication		X		X		
Written communication			X		X	
Leadership	X			X		X
Sensitivity	X			X		X
Initiative			X	X		
Analysis and problem solving		X			X	
Information gathering		X				
Planning and organising	X		X			X
Technical qualifications		X			X	
	3	4	3	4	3	3

Key:
BI = Biographical interview   GD = Group discussion
SI = Situational interview   Test = Aptitude test
IT = In-tray   PQ = Personality
                              questionnaire

Another issue in this debate is whether the final score the candidate receives at the end of the centre, the Overall Assessment Rating (OAR), must necessarily follow an extensive discussion among the assessors; or whether it suffices simply to sum the assigned ratings without any great discussion.

Both sides of the argument have technical merit but in the end the practices adopted will inevitably reflect needs and circumstances. Hence, the more pressed and the less experienced the assessors, the more highly structured should be the scoring system. Current research would suggest that there is little or no difference between the accuracy of OAR's arrived at by these two methods.

Where the 'clinical discussion' approach is most helpful is on matters connected with the assessee's career and personal development and in the composition of an assessment report that is useful to the assessee. Provision should be made for the writing of such a report that gives, in helpful detail, the assessors' individual and collective assessments of the candidate's performance, together with his or her strengths and development needs. In its composition the personal needs and development of the assessee should be kept constantly in mind.

Standards

Many designers have found it useful to draft provisional standards at the design stage by developing behavioural rating scales (*see*

A generic scale for use with an exercise marking guide

7   **Excellent response**—covers all of the key points fully and adds some valid ones of his own, makes no errors.

6   **Very competent response**—covers all of the key points quite fully, almost no errors.

5   **Above acceptable standard**—covers most of the key points, some fully, few errors.

4   **Minimum acceptable standard**—covers few points though these are important, some errors.

3   **Just fails to meet standards**—covers some but misses main points, gets some wrong.

2   **Clearly fails to meet standards**—covers very few points and incompletely, many errors.

1   **Weak response**—misses all the points, makes many errors.

Chapter 2) and sample answers to represent different levels of performance. A reference point should be defined on each scale that corresponds with 'minimum competence' (just acceptable performance) as illustrated in a general-purpose scale shown on p. 121. Used in conjunction with a marking guide, this sort of scale might be applied to the scoring and evaluation of a situational interview, a fact-finding exercise and most other assessment centre exercises.

The next step in setting the standards is to trial the exercises.

Trialling and fine-tuning

The value and payback of running a pilot centre with real assessors and volunteer assessees cannot be overestimated. It puts the exercises to a very necessary test, allowing the assessors and designer to evaluate all aspects—the administration of the centre, the paper work, the suitability of the exercises and the scoring system, the notional standards, the reasonableness of the demands being made on candidates and, more importantly perhaps, on the assessors. As a result of this validation of the process old exercises are revised and new ones are usually added.

Assessor training

As well as training assessors this activity also allows further standardising of the scoring system. Training usually consists of:

- an introduction to the concept, rationale and history of assessment centres
- a review of the centre's dimensions, exercises and the system and documentation for observing, evaluating and scoring
- live participation of the trainees in playing the roles of assessees and assessors. Or, alternatively, practise with pre-prepared assessment data
- based on the role-plays and practice, a comparison of the ratings given by the trainee assessors, discussions and setting the standards that will be operative when the centre goes live
- final revisions of the centre material
- sometimes, an assessor certification process.

Going live

If the centre is a significant in-company programme, steps must be taken to advise and inform candidates, potential candidates and their supervisors so that they can prime themselves, think through their own aspirations, understand the nomination process and work through the personal implications. If a new assessment centre programme runs counter to prevailing practices and expectations about how promotion works then launching it on an unsuspecting organisation can create major shock waves. An extensive communication campaign and a policy of openness should be the order of the day. Whatever the nature and purpose of the centre, advance notice should be provided to assessees describing:

- its objectives
- the uses to be made of the results
- the general nature of the exercises
- the amount of time involved and the timing of selection decisions and feedback
- what is in it for them.

The records of the assessment programme candidates must be retained and monitored to ensure that standards are consistently maintained, that individual assessors are performing satisfactorily and that the centre is continuing to meet the organisation's objectives. Over the course of time, assessors move to new positions and exercises become worn and widely known by potential assessees, hence there is a continuous need for new assessor training and the design of new exercises.

A description of how the Greater Manchester Police Force is using assessment to achieve an equitable balance between the organisation's staffing requirements and the career interests of its officers follows. One of the intended objectives of the programme is to give officers confidence in the fairness and objectivity of the promotion system, hence the choice of the assessment centre method.

Getting it right: The Greater Manchester Police Promotion Assessment System

By 1989 the force had stockpiled enough qualified officers to satisfy the need for sergeants for the next 7 years and inspectors for the next 5 years. This meant that an officer could be 'qualified' for promotion for many years without ever advancing to the higher rank. It also meant that the promotion route was effectively blocked by this log-jam. A similar pattern existed at more senior levels.

Late that year a new system came into effect under the leadership of the Deputy Chief Constable. This is a three-stage process that operates at all ranks up to and including Chief Superintendent. First, candidates for promotion must succeed in nine job tasks set and evaluated by their superior officers over a 12 month period. Next, they must be successful in a rigorous assessment centre, including aptitude testing, where they compete against both an absolute standard and their peers. Those who are ranked highest are advanced to a senior board for selection and placement. By streamlining the assessment process in this way, successful candidates are guaranteed promotion within 18 months.

The assessment centre is the tap which effectively controls the flow to match manpower supply with demand. Candidates and officers alike see this new system as much more objective and fair. External candidates must compete on the same terms as internal candidates.

Further issues to consider

Cost

Assessment centres are usually fairly costly to develop and operate. Apart from the involvement of design consultants the manpower resources required for the various steps are not inconsiderable. For a smaller organisation it would usually be more economical to send individual assessees to a publicly offered assessment centre.

Length of assessor training

While the available research evidence suggests that the validity of assessment centres is unrelated to how long the course lasts, common sense would suggest that assessors must receive a minimum amount of training to be effective. For a one-day centre I have found that training the assessors takes one and a half to two days followed by an additional reorientation and reading-in session immediately before the first live centre. Should assessors fall out of practice a reorientation session is necessary. It is essential to train assessors on any new exercises that are introduced into the centre.

Use of paper-and-pencil tests

Psychological tests are eschewed by more orthodox designers of assessment centres but incorporated into their centres by other more iconoclastic designers. This appears to be more a matter of individual experience and preference than a theoretical issue. Research has shown that both methods of assessment, assessment centre and psychological testing, make a unique contribution in predicting potential and can profitably be used together.

Dimensions vs exercises as basis of evaluation ratings

Other research has shown that the ratings of assessees' performance tend to be highly intercorrelated *within* an exercise and less so *between* exercises. So, for example, the competence of 'planning ability' might be correlated more with 'oral ability', as assessed in a situational interview, than with planning as assessed in an in-tray exercise. Based on this evidence some designers view competence dimensions as an unnecessary complication, omit dimensions from their centres, and have assessors simply assess and evaluate the assessees' performance on the exercise itself. Once again there are pros and cons in both approaches and either is acceptable. One advantage of the dimension-based approach is that a company-wide system of competence dimensions provides a linkage between the assessment centres and other elements of the human resource management system. They also give assessors, assessees and managers a common currency for discussing selection, performance, and development.

10 Behind the scenes

Key points

- *Recruiting and promoting talented people does not depend simply on having good selection tools and skills. The manager must be able to establish the necessary organisational support.*
- *Critically, roles and responsibilities for the various recruitment, assessment and selection activities should be clearly understood and agreed by the line and staff, head office and field. Budget planning, based on manpower forecasts and realistic costing are also required parts of the assessment infrastructure.*
- *The traditional assignment of organisational responsibilities bears re-examination following recent shifts in the roles played by line and Personnel in the management of human resources. Greater expertise in the management of recruitment and assessment is required from both.*
- *To take advantage of assessment technology, smaller organisations must invest in training, contract specialist skills from outside and join with other business organisations to validate their methods.*
- *When used selectively, business psychologists and other specialist consultants can add value to the assessment and selection process.*

Recruiting and promoting people with the best available talents is not merely a matter of analysing the required skills and abilities, or of choosing the best method and training the assessors. Much as these steps are important, they can only be put into action if the underlying structure and resources are coherently organised and are being managed harmoniously. This is particularly true as an organisation grows in size and as roles and responsibilities within it become more and more specialised. Interpersonal issues often arise and must be resolved if managers and staff are to get on with the business of recruiting and promoting capable people.

This chapter looks at what can go wrong in this regard and how to set it right.

Organisational obstacles to good assessment practice

Certain conditions and practices within organisations are known to frustrate good assessment practice in both the public and private sectors. The main problems fall into four categories.

Role and responsibility conflicts

Line and staff roles are not well defined or understood; responsibility is so diffused that important tasks slip between the organisational cracks. Power conflicts arise between the line and the personnel functions, or between warring groups at corporate and divisional levels.

One of the consequences of line-staff friction is the disinclination of an organisation's personnel staff to take risks. Being handy scapegoats for bad selection decisions, there is sometimes a tendency to look for reasons to reject candidates, rather than for positive strengths or signs of potential. This can be a particularly serious problem in times of manpower supply shortage.

Budget, planning and control issues

Provisions made for forthcoming recruitment and assessment are sometimes inadequate due to:

- poor forecasting and planning of manpower requirements
- inadequate costing of the various elements

- failure to anticipate and allow for the temporary assignment of internal manpower to assessment activities
- short-sighted belief that assessment is a safe activity for cost savings.

Lack of expertise

A lack of understanding and skills on the parts of both line and personnel can be a serious handicap. In the past it has not been uncommon for the Personnel department to be relegated as the organisation's 'Cinderella' to a low-level administrative role with a consequent loss of the professional expertise that this department ought to bring to every aspect of recruitment, assessment and selection. A second shortcoming is that very little management training is on offer on how to organise, plan and execute recruitment and assessment projects.

Differing priorities and perspectives

Another cause of poor assessment management is the wide differences in the priorities and perspectives of line managers and personnel specialists. When they are planning and organising a recruitment or promotion project, managers are usually most concerned about:

- how much time and resources it will take
- when they can squeeze it into a diary that is already over committed
- how quickly they can bring people on board before their manpower budget starts to be chopped
- when they can have additional people to share the workload and ease the burden of already overloaded staff
- what they can do to avoid hiring a trouble-maker
- why they have to put up with personnel people who keep getting in the way and complicating things unnecessarily.

Personnel staff, on the other hand, are more likely to be concerned about:

- implementing the processes of assessment and selection with high professional standards

- managing the volumes of paperwork, correspondence and records that are generated by most recruitment projects
- the reliability and validity of the selection methods
- complying with equal employment and race relations legislation
- avoiding criticism from the line about screening in unsuitable candidates
- line managers who seem to be completely deaf to reason and who want to have everything done yesterday.

With widely different concerns, often conflicting in what they see as important, managers and personnel specialists sometimes have great difficulty working in cooperative partnership with one another.

Some of the effects of an inadequate assessment infrastructure are highlighted by the case described below. Not only has the corporate Personnel department been kept strictly at arm's length by the operating divisions, it also lacked the necessary expertise to give sound advice.

Getting it wrong

A senior personnel manager was seeking advice on a resourcing problem. His organisation is a UK television company which enjoys a deserved reputation for the quality of its productions. There was no central department responsible for assessment and the operating departments jealously guarded their independence from the corporate personnel group. In recruiting creative individuals to train as top production staff, manager-producers were finding it difficult to assess for creativity and self-awareness. They were also hoping to select team leaders who would be able to develop the individual creativity of the staff while knitting them into cooperative production teams.

Further examination of the issues revealed several root problems:

- planning for recruitment and selection was entirely hit-and-miss
- job specifications and explicit criteria for assessment and

---

selection did not exist for any of the positions—creativity and leadership meant different things to different producers

- this shortcoming in job specifications had been singled out for special criticism by a race relations tribunal investigating the company's promotion practices
- the traditional board interview was the only assessment method; psychometric tests were rejected as 'too mechanistic'; the use of assessment centres for identifying supervisory talent was a closed book
- interview skills were acquired through live 'practice' and by observing more experienced colleagues, the merits of which were extremely doubtful since the latter had no more training than the tyros
- there was a widely held belief that questions should be wholly hypothetical to elicit creative responses and a candidate's life experience doing creative tasks and managing creative people seems, sadly, to have been ignored
- board interviews were at best loosely structured, the questions and how the interview was carried out being left to the personal standards and biases of the individual interviewers
- managers tended to rush quickly to judgement, then use the balance of the interview to rationalise first impressions
- managers had great difficulty evaluating and integrating interview findings into a coherent view of the candidate
- there was no budget for interview training and, in any event, no training could be offered because the demand for it would have been overwhelming!

Laying the organisational foundations for successful selection

Roles and responsibilities

Who should be directly involved in the management and the operation of assessment-selection and what should their roles be?

Traditional division of responsibility

Line managers would traditionally be responsible for:

- recruitment and assessment budgets (sometimes)
- the final-stage interviews
- the choice of job-skill tests and, sometimes, psychological tests
- final selection and promotion decisions
- induction and management of the successful candidate once appointed.

Traditionally the Personnel department would be responsible for:

- recruitment and assessment budgets (sometimes)
- organising recruitment drives
- managing the assessment and selection process
- handling all the underlying administrative apparatus— including correspondence with applicants and candidates
- selecting, purchasing, administering and scoring psychological tests
- screening applications and conducting preliminary interviews
- resourcing special expertise as required by contracting in
- where Personnel had credibility and a strong presence, advising on senior promotions and succession plans
- where Personnel have credibility and a strong presence, advising the Board on policy issues and systems for recruitment and assessment.

Despite the heavy involvement of the Personnel department, line managers typically 'own' the process.

Clearly, this is not a significant issue for small organisations which are characterised more by a role flexibility born of necessity than by any distinct segmentation of roles. But it is an issue for organisations that have grown and have had to differentiate their organisational structures. In the traditional scheme of things, the Personnel department of enlightened organisations has influenced assessment and selection at the two levels of corporate policy and operating practice. On the policy front, Personnel make presentations and recommend policy on human resource matters to the Board. Once adopted by the Board the policy is then disseminated and put into practice by the line management. Administratively, the Personnel department writes procedures and guidelines, provides support training and, where a centralised approach makes sense, handles much of the administration for recruitment and promotion. A typical breakdown of responsibilities in a traditional structure is given on page 131. Provided that they are clearly defined and supported by a disciplined corporate management there is a lot to be said for this traditional way of organising and balancing line and staff roles.

Re-packaging roles and responsibilities

While there is nothing much wrong with traditional good practice the manager-assessor might wish to re-examine the organisation of responsibilities for possible gains in efficiency and effectiveness. The partition of responsibilities opposite is intended to be illustrative rather than prescriptive.

Depending on the organisation's size and structure all three activities might be decentralised or centralised. It would seem prudent to delegate the Operating activity to the operating departments of the organisation. In a division or a big department a single line manager might have general responsibility for this activity with others being involved both as internal 'customers' and as interviewers and assessors.

Because of the specialised knowledge required by the Assessment Consulting and the Recruitment activity bundles, these would most appropriately reside within the Personnel department and probably at the corporate level. For small and medium-sized organisations it might be cost-effective to contract in consulting

Activity bundles for organising recruitment, assessment and selection

Operating activity bundle

- identifies and forecasts manpower and skills required to meet the operating plan
- manages and controls all budgets
- conducts job analysis
- manages and resources the assessment programmes
- makes selection decisions and offers employment
- gives assessment feedback to candidates
- maintains supplies of assessment materials
- maintains secure records of assessment.

Assessment Consulting activity bundle

- assessment policy advice to the Board
- consults and advises on job analysis, methods and the design of assessment plans
- advises and trains those responsible for the *Operating* activity
- gives interpretations and feedback on advanced psychological tests
- designs and evaluates assessment centres and other methods for the organisation.

Recruitment activity bundle

- gives recruitment policy advice to the Board
- manages human resource planning
- manages recruitment planning
- identifies and monitors labour markets, supplies and demographic trends
- handles recruitment advertising
- receives applications and schedules candidates for assessment
- communicates with candidates.

resources to handle all or some of the Assessment Consulting activities.

However these activities are packaged and however responsibility for them is assigned, it is vital for an organisation's managers to take them in hand and consciously manage them.

Budgeting

Realistic forecasting and planning of manpower requirements, and their ongoing communication to those charged with recruitment, are of the essence. Chapter 11 places this in the context of an integrated system of human resource management. As it is never possible to forecast requirements with precision, allowance needs to be made in the budget for unplanned contingencies.

The costing issue is one that can be handled and updated only at the level of the individual organisation and programme. The checklist of items that follows is offered as a rough-and-ready aid for managers who are building an assessment and selection budget for the first time. The list should of course be extended to include recruitment costs and other items as appropriate for local requirements. As a first cut, the extended version of the checklist may be applied to each and every category of job positions where vacancies have been forecast within each department or division in the organisation. Once this has been done the fixed overheads, duplications and savings can be identified and the whole consolidated into a single budget.

In building an assessment budget, one cannot take for granted the managers and staff from the line who are expected to participate in an assessment activity as content experts, assessors or interviewers. Even though no direct costs may be incurred, their time away from their main responsibilities is a real cost to the organisation and a likely inconvenience for their owning manager. This is something that should be raised in advance and negotiated with the latter.

Some cost items for building an assessment and selection budget

Design costs

- consulting contracts
- assessment materials (e.g., psychological tests) for trialling
- computing time and associated clerical resources for evaluation research
- support staff for typing, photocopying, general clerical work
- involvement of in-house staff as 'content experts' and as guinea pigs.

Operating costs

- non-reusable assessment materials
- non-reusable software programmes for administering or scoring assessment tests
- training of test administrators
- training of interviewers and assessors
- temporary administrative staff
- contract interviewers
- specialist consultants
- rental of rooms for interviews, assessment centre, candidate waiting
- rental of video recording or other equipment
- postage and telephone for communications with candidates
- out-of-pocket expenses for candidates.

General overhead and maintenance

- permanent professional and administrative staff
- dedicated space for offices, storage and assessment
- secure computing facilities for the storage, computation and retrieval of assessment information
- library of technical books and manuals
- licences for specified tests and other assessment materials.

Expertise

Management competence and its ingredients has been a widely discussed and sometimes hotly debated topic in the business and management development media of the late 1980s and the 1990s. Few can argue that getting talented people in the right job, at the right time, is one of the most crucial competences of the professional manager. And for that he or she needs to be able to:

■ build a supporting organisational infrastructure
■ recognise and exploit the knowledge of the specialist
■ plan and execute assessment projects that run smoothly and efficiently
■ understand the tools of assessment, what they cost and, more importantly, what they can do
■ carry out searching interviews that yield reliable and valid evidence about a candidate's suitability for job and team
■ evaluate and control the operation to ensure the quality of the results.

Assessment and selection in smaller organisations

Smaller organisations have generally experienced the greatest difficulty in systematising their assessment and selection processes and taking advantage of the available psycho-technology to improve their practices. Their lack of specialist resources as well as the competing demands on managers' attention have a lot to do with this. The following suggestions might be profitably taken up by the small business manager who can see the potential in having more professional assessment practices.

Pointing line managers in the right direction

Probably the two measures that would have the most immediate impact would be to:

■ give every manager a one-day general course on how to manage assessment in a business-like and professional manner—this

should be tailored to in-company practices and work flows
■ introduce some simple forms and guidelines for use by managers at their discretion—obviously these should make his or her
job easier and not add to the bureaucratic burden.

Job analysis

Implement a simple multi-purpose procedure for carrying out a
job analysis with pre-formatted questionnaires, guides and standard lists of competences.

Training

All managers should have at least a working knowledge of systematic interviewing linked to the standard competence lists. At least
two to three days of training on the job analysis process and in
interviewing should be budgeted for managers who have responsibility for hiring and promotion.

Psychological testing

A responsible member of the administrative staff should receive
training on the basics of test administration concentrating on
relatively simple ability and skill tests. The person elected must
have top management's authority to establish the standards and to
control all uses of testing in the organisation. It would be wise to
retain an indpendent occupational psychologist for advice as and
when needed.

Middle manager assessment

When needing to assess candidates for middle management positions the small organisation might consider either in-depth psychological assessment or a public assessment centre. Both types of
service are offered by a number of external consultants.

Graduate recruitment

There are consultancies that offer screening interviewing and a
comprehensive battery of psychological testing.

Selection of top managers

Regardless of its size, an organisation would be wise to consider an independent in-depth psychological assessment by a reputable business psychologist.

Validation research

If the numbers of employees or new hires is too small to permit research, then there is a case for joining with others in a consortium to establish and maintain properly validated assessment methods. The various management institutes that represent the smaller businesses could do their members a great deal of service by sponsoring such research.

Consultants

A number of organisations in the private and public sectors regularly commission consulting psychologists who are expert in assessment and selection. In general, the more critical it is for an organisation to make the right hiring or promotion decision, the more valuable will be the services of a consulting psychologist. Managers will find that working in partnership with a business or occupational psychologist is particularly useful when:

- setting up a new assessment-selection system
- introducing a systematic approach for job analysis into the organisation or conducting a large-scale job analysis
- designing a sophisticated assessment procedure, such as an assessment centre
- considering the use or actually using any kind of psychological test or questionnaire for selection or promotion, but particularly personality instruments
- training resident managers or staff on assessment procedures or giving feedback
- assessing a candidate for a senior management position.

Usually only large organisations can afford to employ expert staffing specialists and fewer yet have resident psychologists.

There are numerous consultancies offering the necessary advice and services, though caution must be exercised to ensure that the level of expertise claimed is genuine. Vetting prospective consultants is a thorny problem for organisational managers who have little direct experience. In the UK the British Psychological Society's chartering of qualified psychologists gives a measure of quality assurance. When selecting a psychologist the manager should always ensure that the chartered psychologist has training or experience in personnel assessment and selection.

The IPM qualification granted by the Institute of Personnel Management is also a respected credential, though by itself it does not guarantee that the holder is qualified to consult on assessment and selection. Once again the prospective client needs to evaluate the individual consultant on his or her own merits.

11 A systematic overview

Key points

- *When establishing a supporting organisational infrastructure, it is useful to think of assessment and selection as part of a human resource management system the object of which is to supply on time the manpower necessary to meet the organisation's goals.*
- *The organisation's strategic and operational plans are the starting point. All the constituent processes, including human resource planning, recruitment, assessment and selection, induction and training, and performance appraisal, are in the service of those plans.*
- *To manage the assessment-selection activity effectively it is necessary to monitor key indicators, such as: the number of applicants, selection ratios at the various stages, rejection rates, and variances from planned intake figures.*
- *Mechanisms may be set up to monitor recruitment/promotion statistics and practices for signs of illegal discrimination against protected groups and unfair discrimination against any other minorities. Other considerations aside, discriminatory practices block important sources of manpower.*
- *Organisations should be checking the reliability and validity of their assessment tools to ensure they are delivering competent manpower. This means conducting validation studies.*

In some organisations selection and promotion are isolated events set in motion whenever a vacancy or vacancies occur. Once the vacancy is filled nothing much else happens as a result of the assessment and the information gathered during the process is shredded or filed, never to be seen again. After induction, sadly, there is rarely any follow-up to correct skill deficiencies identified in the assessment. And little or no effort is made to evaluate the accuracy of the assessment process against the later performance of those who were hired or promoted.

A framework for assessment and selection

There are distinct advantages in viewing assessment and selection in connection with other related activities, like career development and training, rather than as isolated events. Interconnectedness would mean that information about an individual's particular strengths and limitations gathered during his or her recruitment would not be discarded but used to formulate a personalised development plan.

Another advantage of taking a 'connected' view could be a common language of concepts used across the organisation to describe abilities and performance in all the various sub-systems of human resource management. So the competence dimensions on which recruits were assessed could be the same ones that are used to assess their subsequent performance or to identify their training needs. A common language makes it easier for members of the organisation to communicate with one another and it fosters consistency in the ways that people are evaluated.

But perhaps the main advantages in interconnected processes lie in the setting of objectives and the planning of human resourcing activities. In organisations which have a systematic approach, assessment and selection are viewed within the broader context of human resource management as elements in a more or less integrated system for managing and developing the organisation's human resources. Together with training, management development, career and succession planning, they are the means whereby the system supplies the qualified people it needs to sustain itself and to grow. Page 143 shows an idealised picture of how the sub-systems are related to one another. As well as illustrating the advantages of an integrated perspective it offers an orienting framework for planning an organisation's resourcing activities.

Planning

One of the aims of the human resource system is to ensure that new recruits, internal as well as external, are closely matched, in number, skills and age to the organisation's forthcoming business requirements. The starting point of the assessment and selection process, therefore, is the parent organisation's strategic and operating plans.

Manpower projections from the strategic and operating plans are input to a human resourcing planning process which serves to regulate the numbers and types of personnel entering or cycled through the organisation. Other kinds of input into this process include manpower profiles, succession and career plans, and macro analysis of training and development needs.

Strong lines of communication must be maintained between those charged with human resource planning on the one hand and recruitment and assessment on the other to allow sufficient time to mount a recruitment campaign and assessment project.

In recruitment planning, the process of projecting the required numbers and mix of full-time workers, freelances, temporary staff and sub-contracted labour for the projected occupational vacancies. Due account must be taken of seasonal factors, demographic patterns and trends, skill availability, and wage and salary comparisons. The recruitment plan triggers one or more recruitment projects. Maintaning ties with universities, colleges and local schools, and participating in recruitment fairs is an important secondary role of the recruitment planner.

Recruitment

Systems, processes and methods of recruitment will not be treated here in any detail. They have been extensively covered in other published sources. Some of the main elements of the recruitment process are: a targeted market (internal or external), a campaign plan to attract promising applications, an advertising medium, application forms or some other way to receive applications, and planned dates that reflect the required turnaround times.

Assessment and selection in a human resource management system

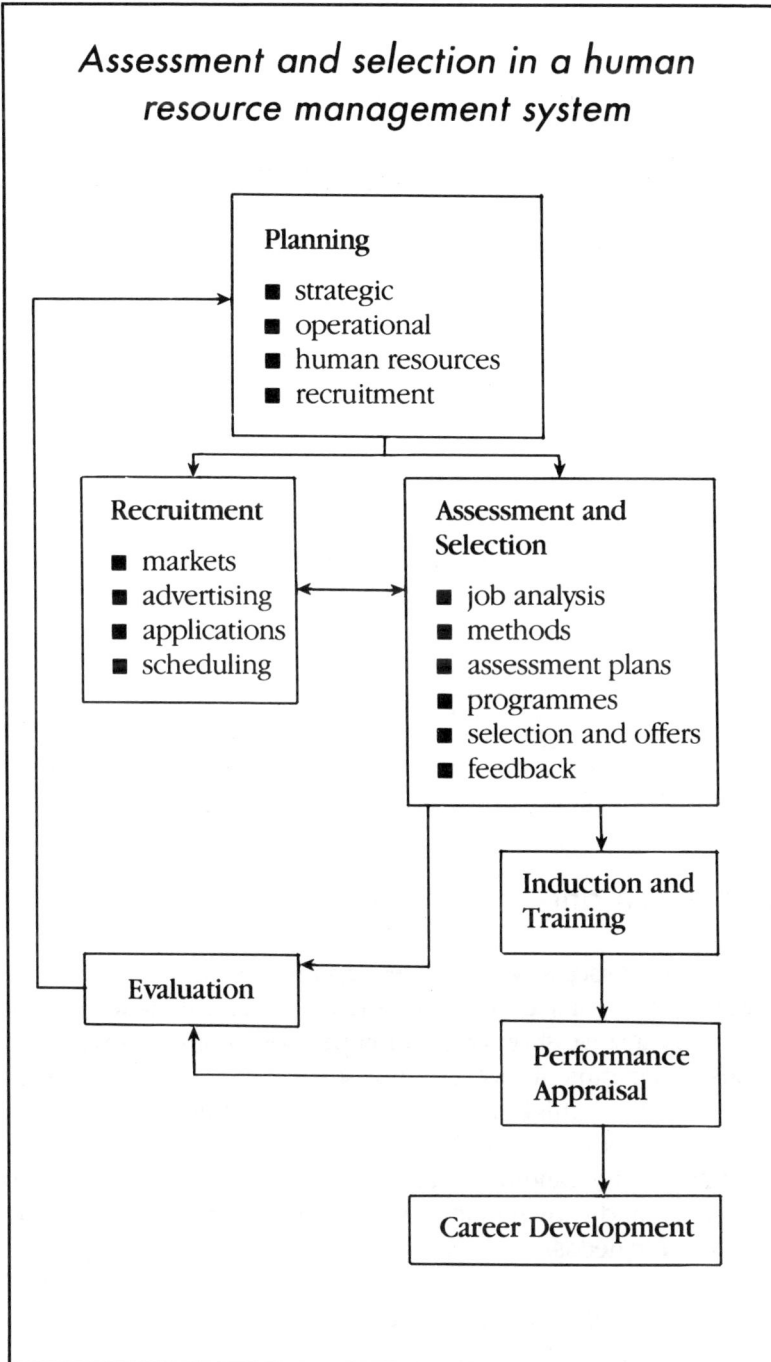

Planning
- strategic
- operational
- human resources
- recruitment

Recruitment
- markets
- advertising
- applications
- scheduling

Assessment and Selection
- job analysis
- methods
- assessment plans
- programmes
- selection and offers
- feedback

Induction and Training

Evaluation

Performance Appraisal

Career Development

Assessment and selection

The identification of human resource requirements during planning should trigger a process for analysing the jobs targeted by the strategic/operating plans (*see* Chapter 2). Once job dimensions and criteria are specified and defined a choice is then made of the assessment methods best suited to these requirements and purposes (*see* Chapter 3).

Planning an assessment means defining the various selection stages and the sequence in which they will take place (*see* Chapter 4). It is at this point that ground rules are set on how candidates' results are to be interpreted at each stage. It is also at this point that the assessors are usually briefed and, if required, trained on how to handle their assessment role and tasks.

Following the assessment programme, decisions are made on which candidates to select or promote and the necessary appointment machinery is set in motion. Typically this entails issuing a, usually, written offer conditional on receipt of a satisfactory medical report and references. If these are satisfactory, the offer is confirmed and a contract of employment is signed.

Once in position the appointee receives feedback about the assessment findings. His or her development needs may be identified and plans made for meeting them. Assessment feedback may also be offered to unsuccessful candidates as well.

Induction and training

This is the process whereby new appointees find out about the organisation, their department, their roles and their work team. This may involve short orientation periods in different work sections or departments. Job training, sometimes spread over a fairly extended time, might also be given. If the assessment has been closely related to the requirements of the job, the emerging pattern of a successful candidate's strengths and weaknesses will allow induction and early training to be tailored more closely to his or her specific needs.

Performance appraisal

The initial performance appraisal meeting between new appointees and their supervisors is the first step of the performance management process. Its chief purpose is to communicate the results the former is expected to achieve and in what time frame. Subsequent performance reviews and discussions are held to evaluate results and give performance feedback. Many organisations use a formalised procedure to rate performance. Again, the individual's results from the assessment-selection should be valuable grist to this particular mill and, together with the output from ongoing performance appraisal, inform the whole career development process.

Evaluation and validation

Evaluation has several different aspects involving different indicators and mechanisms, some involving the validity of the assessment tools, others the organisation's objectives, and yet others the reactions of the participants. Before going operational with a new assessment-selection system or programme, it is a good idea to determine what key indicators will be tracked and evaluated, and to make adequate provision for monitoring them. The following could be used.

Applicant numbers

This is an obvious indicator. If the number of applicants should drop significantly the causes should be explored and identified—an unexpected demographic shift, a competitor fishing in the same pool with better bait or a flaw in the advertising or the recruitment campaign. With appropriate corrective action taken, it might be prudent then to extend the recruitment pool to non-traditional groups, just as a number of companies have done with older recruits, and to adjust the assessment methods accordingly.

Selection ratios

The selection ratio is the proportion of successful candidates to the total number of candidates passing through at each stage of a particular assessment programme. Any noticeable deviation from what is customary or anticipated could indicate a number of things that should be checked: a significant change in the type of people applying, quality assurance problems among the assessors, loss of security of the assessment methods or administrative error.

Rejections

An indicator that managers neglect at their peril is the percentage of rejected offers. A lower than expected take-up rate by external candidates could indicate either superior offers from competing employers, or a flaw in candidate care and public relations. Rejections by internal applicants for promotion could have any number of interpretations that would need to be investigated urgently.

Managers should also note that internal assessment programmes can have major unintended consequences on staff motivation and morale. Such a result was found in a study of staff reactions to assessment for a fast track development programme in a major UK bank. Staff who failed were likely to feel alienated, to be less committed to work and to be more likely to seek new employment elsewhere. This is an issue where anticipation is unquestionably preferable to after-the-fact monitoring of the problem. In either event, assessment methods should be designed to minimise adverse reactions from candidates who are unsuccessful and to give them as much control and responsibility for the process as possible.

Meeting the business and the human resourcing plans

At all stages of the resourcing process it is necessary to keep sight of the planned targets and to keep checking that new hires and promotions fit the bill. Perhaps the recruitment campaign needs to be revised or the assessment process changed. Of course, the cause of a problem might lie in some other part of the human resource management system—training and development, performance management, the reward system, or the design of the job. If new hires do not seem to be right, therefore, the resource manager would do well to analyse the causes before jumping to an obvious but erroneous solution.

Equal opportunity monitoring

Monitoring compliance with legal requirements for equality of treatment means keeping track of the proportions of candidates, by sex and minority-group membership, who are hired and promoted at all levels and all occupational groups. Keeping these statistics has the added benefit of drawing attention to neglected or under-utilised recruitment sources. So whether the concern is about social duty or merely dwindling recruitment supplies, the manager should be looking particularly at groups which have historically been at the short end of unfair discrimination practices—women, the over-forties, members of racial minorities, single parents and the handicapped. Below is a useful checklist for monitoring abuses against minority candidates published by the Commission for Racial Equality.

A checklist for auditing disproportionate selection of minority candidates

If analysis of selection and promotion ratios reveals that fewer black candidates are successful, check each stage of selection against the following:

1 Do more black applicants lack entry qualifications, experience or skill requirements or fail selection tests? If so can other measures of potential be used which do not have this effect? Would pre- or post-entry training offset lack of experience and assist in spotting potential? If the company runs YTS schemes, or finances any community projects, can they recruit black trainees with potential for these schemes?

2 Are black applicants disproportionately excluded because of preferred age limits, place of residence, dress or uniform requirements, or domestic circumstances? If so, re-examine the need for these.

3 Do more black applicants fail at the interview? Is it because of stereotyping by selectors, or the effects of unconscious attitudes, or self-image selection, or fears about the reactions of colleagues, clients or customers? Selection yard-

sticks may need to be reassessed so that more decisions are made on facts rather than subjective impressions. Selectors may need practical training on how to select fairly and how to avoid racial discrimination. The use of equality targets ... gives selectors a long-term aim, and increases the chances that black applicants will be selected.

4 Do selectors screen out more application forms from people with foreign names or an overseas education?

5 Do selectors misjudge applicants' written and oral English skills? If many younger Asian applicants are rejected because of inadequate English this may well suggest that unfair or inaccurate assessments are being used as they have probably been educated in England.

Reported in *Jobs and Racial Equality* by M. Coussey and J. Whitmore of the Commission for Racial Equality, 1986.

Validity and reliability

As we saw in Chapter 4, an assessment method is considered to be valid if high scorers do relatively well in training, in job performance, or in the promotion stakes—and low scorers do correspondingly poorly on these success measures. We also saw that a method is considered reliable if its results for individual assessees are consistent from one occasion to another. Regrettably, the amount of research into these aspects is less than desirable.

Lack of systematic evaluation of the accuracy and validity of assessment programmes and devices is perhaps symptomatic of the pressures managers are under. For those concerned with fighting today's fires or about the City's reactions to the quarterly figures the question of predicting the future success of today's new appointees may not be a very high priority. For others it might be due to a lack of skill and understanding about validation. It is difficult to know what needs to happen to change this, for without management support validation research cannot be done. Managers should understand that there are real benefits in sponsoring what might at first appear to be rather arcane and academic research. By carrying out systematic programmes to test the validity of their methods for selecting supervisors and managers, companies like Standard Oil and Sears have been able to refine them to a point where they are highly predictive and invaluable management tools.

Conclusion

The point of painting this picture of the human resourcing system has been to underline the place of assessment in the larger scheme of things. The reader who is accustomed to the mud and bullets of the organisational trenches will recognise that this sort of rational representation is idealised rather than real. In practice it is unrealistic to strive for a system in which every process is interconnected with every other process. This may lead to large bureaucratic systems that too often limit the discretion managers need to get things done and, even with the best of intentions, become an end instead of the means to an end.

Nonetheless, it is eminently clear that effective planning and control of manpower resourcing makes a measure of integration essential.

12 Principles for managing assessment

Key points

- *There are a few key underlying principles that apply to the management of assessment and selection: balancing the interests of the organisation and individual; selection on merit; equal opportunity; openness of information; security and confidentiality; job-relatedness; multiple measurement; assessors and selectors who have training and integrity.*
- *Managers intent on improving their organisation's capability might do well to begin with an audit of existing assessment and selection practices.*

What must be done to manage assessment professionally, effectively and in a manner that will continue to serve the organisation's resourcing objectives? In addition to the good practices described in the preceding chapters there are just a few key principles that might be worthy of the manager-assessor's attention. These are summarised here in no particular order of merit.

Balance of organisation and individual interests

An employer has a right and an obligation to its shareholders to hire and deploy human resources in a way that satisfies its legitimate business interests and objectives. On the other hand, the individual candidate and employee has a right to be treated with respect and to have access to employment opportunities, career choice and some security of tenure.

Clearly neither freedom is, or can be, absolute and a balance must be sought to reflect prevailing norms and economic values. In their assessment policies and practices ethical employers strike a just balance between the interests of the organisation and the individual.

Merit-based selection and promotion

To meet its legitimate business needs and the interests of all its stakeholders, the organisation strives to employ and promote those who are the best qualified, the most able and the most highly motivated at a price it can afford. For purposes of selection and promotion, merit is measured against criteria of competence, not by length of service, seniority of qualification, family membership or club affiliation. Few practices do more to sap the commitment of able managers and staff than that of nepotism. Changing the rules in cultures where promotion was once based on nepotism or on time-serving may arouse opposition as the following case illustrates.

Fiddling in Rome

In Rome, competition is so great for public sector jobs-for-life that 28,000 people applied for 100 clerking jobs in the Italian parliament. Traditionally, the entrance examination was invariably circumvented on all sides and appointment to these jobs was governed by family membership rather than by any special ability to do the job. All this was changed and the principle of merit received a much-needed boost with the introduction of new computer-based technology into the assessment. Test security was guaranteed and opportunities for tampering with the scoring were removed by using the computer to randomly select the test questions and an optical scanner to read the completed answer sheets into the computer. The scores that came out had been untouched by human hand. Predictably, not everyone was equally impressed by this revolution in assessment technology. Cars of test invigilators were reportedly vandalised and there was talk of dire retaliative measures among the irate members of the established families.

Equal opportunity

Evidence from research and litigation has shown overwhelmingly that women and people from ethnic minorities are disproportionately and unfairly excluded from job opportunities. Much of this is due to recruitment practices which have in-built biases, such as the 'old boy' network or advertising in newspapers that do not have a minority readership. Ignorance of good assessment and selection practices among managers and staff responsible for screening, assessing, selection and promotion also plays a part. Following good assessment-selection practice counteracts the abuses of discrimination, conscious or otherwise.

Openness of information

Openness refers to the disclosure and dissemination of information about the assessment-selection process. It is also about giving individuals helpful feedback about their assessment results and the career implications. Open disclosure and access to information gives individuals a higher level of control over their future. They can appraise themselves more realistically, rule themselves in or out of contention more appropriately, and make better informed career choices. Giving information before assessment also helps to defuse candidates' anxieties which in turn leads to a more reliable picture of true strengths and capabilities. Organisational secretiveness, the countervalue, disempowers the individual and encourages an undesirable dependence.

Security and confidentiality

Having an open system of assessment does not mean unrestricted access to tests and other assessment materials, or to the assessment information on individuals. For obvious reasons there can be no meaningful assessment unless the security of the former is completely protected. Similarly, stringent measures must be adopted to ensure that all personal assessment results remain confidential. The reputations of candidates, the integrity of the system and the credibility of the managers who run it depend on this.

Job-relatedness of assessment

Practices and standards should closely reflect the demands of the target job and the environmental conditions under which it is performed. The qualities and criteria that are assessed should be bona fide job requirements and the standards applied when selecting candidates should be compatible with the standards required to perform the job to a satisfactory level. Using selection criteria that have little or nothing to do with the job at hand, or applying unrealistically high or unreasonably low standards, all have a predictably negative impact on productivity, job satisfaction and employee turnover.

Multiple measurement

Using a single method to assess a candidate for selection or promotion is a little bit like using a schoolboy's ruler to measure one of Roland Emmett's wonderful contraptions. Each may yield some useful information but will certainly omit many important and interesting aspects. A fuller, more reliable and more useful understanding of a candidate will be gained through the application of several different assessment methods and more than one assessor.

The training and integrity of assessors and selectors

Personnel entrusted with any role in the process of selecting or promoting the human resources of an organisation should be suitably qualified to discharge this responsibility. The disastrous consequences of unskilled amateurism for business profitability and individual success are too serious to entertain.

The next steps

Having seen some of the things that can, and in certain cases should, be done in assessment, the manager is now at a point to take stock of current practices in his or her area of responsibility. The following checklist focuses on the areas highlighted in the preceding pages. If after completing it the manager-assessor is able to identify opportunities to exploit or challenges to overcome, then the ideas found in these chapters will hopefully have provided some of the answers.

A checklist for Managing Assessment

1 Those responsible for recruitment, assessment and selection:

- agree about what is important, they share a common philosophy
- understand and accept the manpower resourcing needs and priorities of the organisation
- work to accepted roles and responsibilities
- place a high value on candidate care
- deliver on their commitments.

2 There is an acceptable level of 'system interface' between assessment-selection activities and:

- human resource planning
- succession planning
- career development
- induction training
- performance management (appraisal) system.

3 Assessment projects are planned and executed to include:

- costing and budgeting provision for each activity
- a defined organisational objective
- a job analysis
- a definition of selection criteria that are job-related, fair and documented in printed form
- any necessary training or briefing for assessors and selectors
- a sequence of selection stages that is efficient and cost effective to run.

4 The assessment tools that are chosen for a project are:

- suitably matched to the required need
- reliable and valid

- administered by suitably trained people
- efficient and cost effective to buy or design, administer and score.

5 Interviews carried out for purposes of selection and promotion are planned in advance so that:

- there is a structure to follow
- the competence criteria have been specified
- interviewers are briefed and know what kinds of questions to ask
- arrangements are made for a quiet room with suitable furniture and lighting
- arrangements are made to invite, inform and greet the candidate.

6 The selection and promotion interviewers:

- follow their plan and cover the intended ground within the scheduled times
- ask searching questions but do not deliberately subject interviewees to stress
- concentrate on behaviour and performance
- review and organise their interview notes immediately following the interview.

7 Any psychological test used for selection and promotion:

- measures an important competence identified by a job analysis
- is supported by a suitable administrative and technical manual
- has at least two parallel forms
- has an objective scoring key or marking guide
- is reliable and valid for the intended use
- has norms suitable for the intended use
- is stored and used under the strictest security
- is administered under carefully controlled conditions free from noise and all other distractions

- is administered, scored and interpreted by people who are trained and qualified to do this.

8 Any assessment centre that is used for selection or promotion:

- is based on a job analysis and simulates important elements of the job
- involves candidates in several exercises for a day or longer
- involves the candidate being assessed by two or more trained assessors
- is managed by a trained administrator
- makes provision for giving feedback to candidates.

9 Assessment programmes and activities are evaluated by:

- monitoring throughput indicators and targets
- monitoring the proportion of minority candidates being selected
- conducting research into the validity of the assessment tools
- surveying candidates' reactions to the assessment experience
- monitoring the costs of all aspects.

10 Candidates are cared for by:

- providing helpful and informative details about the organisation, the job, the assessment-selection process and schedule, directions and timing
- on the day of the assessment greeting them, and explaining arrangements for travel expenses, coffee, meals, waiting areas and toilets
- treating them with courtesy and respect, inviting their questions and providing information
- informing them of the outcomes as quickly as possible
- after the assessment, offering and providing feedback on the psychological tests and assessment centre performance.

APPENDIX 1: A JOB ANALYSIS FORM FOR MANAGEMENT AND SUPERVISORY POSITIONS

ORGANISATIONAL STRUCTURE

1 Job title:_____

2 Current grade:_____

3 Location:_____

4 Department/division:_____

5 Reports to position of:_____

6 Position manager's name:_____

7 Title and grade of highest
   direct subordinate:_____

8 Number of direct reports:_____

9 Total number of reports:_____

10 Number of indirect reports:_____

11 Supervising others from outside
   the organisation:_____

12 Number of other positions the same
   (i.e. title, responsibilities, key results):_____

RESPONSIBILITIES AND ACCOUNTABILITY

13 Direct financial accountability:
   ■ total spend including salaries_____
   ■ total revenue_____
   ■ profit contribution_____

14 Primary mandate:_____
   _____
   _____

15 Main responsibilities:
   ■ _____
     _____
   ■ _____
     _____
   ■ _____
     _____
   ■ _____
     _____

■ _____

16   Expected results and outcomes:

■ _____

■ _____

■ _____

■ _____

■ _____

GENERAL CONDITIONS

17   Number of hours worked in typical week:

_____

18   Business travel:
   ■ number of trips annually_____
   ■ usual duration of trip_____

19   Nature of the work:
   Routine   follows established procedures with no requirement or discretion to adjust
   □   them
   Complex   individual cases/tasks have complexities/nuances requiring problem solv-
   □   ing/interpretation
   Varied   work is rarely the same; conditions or priorities are unpredictable or uncer-
   □   tain
   Project   work is assigned in specific areas of concentration with set objectives and
   □   definite end points
   Other   _____

   _____

20   Degree of supervision:
   Close   □   work is continually monitored and checked
   Moderate   □   work is checked regularly on a predetermined schedule
   Minimal   □   job-holder keeps supervisor advised and is rarely checked
   Independent   □   works within own discretion and decision-making authority

21   Unusual physical job conditions:
   ■ demands (sitting, carrying, lifting, walking etc.)

   _____

   _____

   _____

■ environmental conditions (pollutants, temperature etc.)

_____

_____

_____

ENVIRONMENTAL FORCES

22 Stability of position (i.e. unchanging, recently created, recently changed, how it has changed, organisational reactions to any change):

_____

_____

_____

23 In-company changes likely to impact the job:

_____

_____

_____

24 External changes likely to impact the job:

_____

_____

_____

25 Resources:
■ resources other than budgets and people

_____

_____

■ constraints or limitations on resources

_____

_____

26 Likely problems and stresses (for an average person):

_____

_____

27 Typical dislikes (things frequently disliked by job-holders):

_____

_____

WORKING RELATIONSHIPS

28 Main stakeholders (others who have vested interest in job holder's performance—customers, other departments etc.):

_____

_____

_____

29   Job boundaries and relationships with other units in the organisation:

_____

_____

_____

30   Job boundaries and relationships with other organisations from outside the organisation:

_____

_____

_____

31   Values, attitudes and abilities of significant others which are likely to impact the position:

_____

_____

_____

APPENDIX 2: A CHECKLIST OF GENERAL OCCUPATIONAL SKILLS

DIRECTIONS

On entry to a job the individual job-holder must be able to perform certain tasks otherwise the job doesn't get done, is done badly or someone else has to do it. The employing organisation may provide training for certain of the necessary skills shortly after entry. If it does so then there is little need to assess for the skills that are to be trained. The skills the analyst must identify are the ones which are the most critical to job effectiveness and which a person must bring at entry into the job. Having done this he or she then devises an assessment plan that specifies which skills are to be assessed and by what means.

1 Start by circling the numbers of the skill items which are part of the job being analysed.

2 Add any other skills that are important to the job and circle them too.

3 Now, in the column headed 'Training provided' and for each one of the circled items, put a tick if the new appointee is to receive the training required to bring him or her to the required skill level. Hereafter, ignore those that you have ticked as 'Training provided'.

4 Turn next to the column headed 'Importance rating'. For each one of the remaining circled items, write a 3 if this skill is critical for effective job performance, a 2 if it is quite important, and a 3 if it's a nice-to-have but not all that critical. From here on, ignore the 3's and give precedence to the 1's.

5 Evaluate if any of the items that are marked 1s and 2s should be ignored. For example, it would be pointless to assess for skills that are in high supply in the population, that is, if virtually everyone has them.

6 Decide how you will assess the remaining items marked 1's and 2's. Write a code corresponding to your chosen means of assessment in the column headed 'Chosen method'.

Here are some suggested codes:

AF = Application form	*SI = Situational interview*
CV = Curriculum vitae	*TI = Technical interview*
BI = Behavioural interview	*WE = Written exercise*
RC = Reference check	*CST = Clerical skill test*
IHT = In-company knowledge test	*PT = Performance test*
AAT = Aptitude, ability test	*GE = Group exercise*

7 Examine the output thoroughly. Can you afford to use all of the chosen methods; does each one add appreciable value relative to its cost? Do you have the staff resources to administer them? If necessary, prioritize the methods that give the greatest weight and concentrate on them.

GENERAL OCCUPATIONAL SKILLS CHECKLIST

Name of analyst: .... Date: ...... / ...... / ......

Organisation: .... Unit: ....

Title of job: ....

Job group: ....

A   ARITHMETIC CALCULATION

Solve number problems requiring addition, subtraction, multiplication or division of the following kind:

Importance rating

Training provided   Chosen method

1 Short
2 Lengthy
3 Compound
4 Fractions
5 Decimals
6 Money
7 Percentages
8 Powers/roots
9 Proportions/ratios
10 Apply a standard formula
11 Metric conversion
12 Currency exchange
13 Weight
14 Time
15 Distance/height/length

A calculator is available:

16 Always
17 Sometimes
18 Never or rarely

B   NUMERICAL ESTIMATION AND REASONING

Solve number problems of the following kind involving the interpretation of numerical concepts, facts or data and the drawing of conclusions or deductions from the interpretation:

Importance rating

Training provided   Chosen method

19 Algebraic equations
20 Distance, speed or time

Importance rating		Training provided	Chosen method
	21 Time or cost estimates		
	22 Financial—general		
	23 Balance sheet, P and L statement		
	24 Stocks and bonds		
	25 Budgets and expenditures		
	26 Exchange rates		
	27 Mathematical modelling		
	28		
	29		
	30		

C   GEOMETRIC CALCULATION AND ESTIMATION

Calculate, measure or estimate angles, shapes, surfaces or volumes:

Importance rating		Training provided	Chosen method
	31 Angles		
	32 Perimeter or area of straight-sided figure		
	33 Perimeter or area of curvilinear figure		
	34 Volume of straight-sided objects		
	35 Volume of curvilinear objects		
	36 Angle or lengths by micrometer		
	37		
	38		

D   CHARTS, GRAPHS, INDUSTRIAL DRAWINGS AND DESIGN

Use, evaluate or make visual representations of objects, plans or data:

Importance rating		Training provided	Chosen method
	39 Read graphs		
	40 Read tables or charts		
	41 Read maps		
	42 Read/work from schematic drawings		
	43 Read/work from drawings/photographs		
	44 Visualise how an object would look from printed assembly instructions		
	45 Read/work from blueprints or scale drawings		
	46 Make graphs or charts		
	47 Make schematic drawings		
	48 Make blueprints		

Importance rating		Training provided	Chosen method
☐	49 Evaluate the design quality of objects	☐	☐
☐	50 Evaluate the design quality of printed material	☐	☐
☐	51		
☐	52		
☐	53		

E   TALKING AND LISTENING

Perform the following communication tasks:

Importance rating		Training provided	Chosen method
☐	54 Give or receive simple routine instructions or information orally	☐	☐
☐	55 Give or receive detailed/complex instructions or information orally	☐	☐
☐	56 Routine use of the telephone	☐	☐
☐	57 Use of telephone to persuade others	☐	☐
☐	58 Give instructions or information to people in groups	☐	☐
☐	59 Obtain information by questioning	☐	☐
☐	60 Talk persuasively to customers, suppliers or significant others	☐	☐
☐	61 Prepare and make oral presentations	☐	☐
☐	62 Speak clearly for safety reason	☐	☐
☐	63 Speak with good grammar and pronunciation for business reason	☐	☐
☐	64 Listen and understand what is intended by interpreting behaviour of another	☐	☐
☐	65		
☐	66		
☐	67		

F   READING

Read, understand and interpret printed or written information of the following kinds:

Importance rating		Training provided	Chosen method
☐	68 Factual information in simple forms and notices	☐	☐
☐	69 Simple reports or manuals	☐	☐
☐	70 Complex reports, manuals, articles or books	☐	☐
☐	71		
☐	72		
☐	73		

G WRITTEN COMMUNICATION

Perform the following written tasks:

Importance
rating   Training Chosen
                                                                        provided method

74 Fill out forms with words or phrases
75 Compose notes, short memos or routine letters
76 Compose factual reports or letters of some complexity or judgement
77 Observe events and organise and record them in a written report
78 Edit and correct written material to clarify/improve style
79 Edit and correct written material with judgement and discretion
80 Compose tactful or diplomatic letters or memos
81 Write with grammar and spelling at the following level:
 ■ advanced (broadsheet newspaper)
 ■ average (GCSE or O' Level)
 ■ basic (communicates meaning)
82
83
84

H COMPUTING AND KEYBOARDING

Perform the following tasks using a typewriter, a PC or mainframe keyboard, a printer or another similar device:

Importance
rating   Training Chosen
                                                                        provided method

85 Operate an electric typewriter
86 Operate the following: Micro, PC, work station, or word
    processing terminal at the level indicated:
 ■ ....
 ■ advanced, instructs others
 ■ fully competent
 ■ working knowledge
 ■ learning stage
87 Type notes, memos, simple letters, forms or bulletins
88 Type reports or letters at the following rate and accuracy
 ■ 70+ words per minute
 ■ 60+ words per minute
 ■ 50+ words per minute
 ■ 40+ words per minute
 ■ 30+ words per minute
89 Plan and type tables or graphs

Importance rating		Training provided	Chosen method

90 Operate the following word processing programme at level indicated:
- ....
- advanced, instructs others
- fully competent
- working knowledge
- learning stage

91 Use the following data-base programme at the level indicated:
- ....
- advanced, instructs others
- fully competent
- working knowledge
- learning stage

92 Use the following spreadsheet programme at the level indicated:
- ....
- advanced, instruct others
- fully competent
- working knowledge
- learning

93 Use the following data-base programme at the level indicated:
- ....
- advanced, instructs others
- fully competent
- working knowledge
- learning stage

94 Use the following specified programme at the level indicated:
- ....
- advanced, instructs others
- fully competent
- working knowledge
- learning stage

95 Use DOS at the level indicated:
- ....
- advanced, instructs others
- fully competent
- working knowledge
- learning stage

96 Use OS-2 at the level indicated:
- ....
- advanced, instructs others
- fully competent
- working knowledge
- learning stage

I CLERICAL

Perform the following tasks:

Importance rating		Training provided	Chosen method
☐	97 Sort and file printed materials following a set procedure	☐	☐
☐	98 Sort or classify parts, tools, equipment or products	☐	☐
☐	99 Set up lists or categories for sorting or classifying information or objects	☐	
☐	100 Retrieve files by category code		
☐	101 Proofread printed/written material		
☐	102 Compare lists of numbers, letters or words for differences		
☐	103		
☐	104	☐	☐

J DEALING WITH PROBLEMS

Identify, analyse and solve problems by performing the following tasks:

Importance rating		Training provided	Chosen method
☐	105 Recognise that a problem, fault or hazard exists and identify its likely source	☐	☐
☐	106 Gather information about the nature of the problem, fault or hazard	☐	
☐	107 Analyse causes, looking for cause and effect		
☐	108 Figure out alternative ways of solving a problem or correcting a fault		
☐	109 Test out different solutions to find the best one		
☐	110 Make recommendations about solutions		
☐	111 Devise a creative plan or idea		
☐	112 Implement the plan or idea		
☐	113 Contribute to group problem-solving		
☐	114		
☐	115	☐	☐

(Continued)

K   LEARNING

Acquire the following understanding, skill, knowledge or ability in respect of the job and its context that will enable the job-holder to achieve the desired results:

Importance rating		Training provided	Chosen method
☐	116		
☐	117	☐	☐
☐	118	☐	☐
☐	119	☐	☐
☐	120	☐	☐
☐	121	☐	☐
☐	122	☐	☐
☐	123	☐	☐
☐	124	☐	☐
☐	125	☐	☐

APPENDIX 3: A LIST OF GENERAL MANAGEMENT AND SUPERVISORY COMPETENCES

DIRECTIONS: *Adapt the directions for the General Occupational Skills.*

I Personal

1 Self-confidence
Has a strong but realistic belief in him/herself and his/her ability to accomplish a goal.

2 Positive outlook
His/her views and expectations of the future are optimistic, though realistic and feasible.

3 Achievement motive
Habitually driven to achieve high standards of excellence and success.

4 Independent initiative
Is self-reliant, initiates action without needing or awaiting direction from others.

5 Adaptability and resilience
Adapts successfully to changes in life, business and organisational environment.

6 Critical analysis
Breaks an event into its elements, extracting the essential assumptions and facts, and deducing causes and effects.

7 Balanced judgement
As well as considering rational argument and hard fact, reflects on his/her own values and the needs and feelings of others when selecting a course of action.

8 Decision handling
Is ready to commit to a timely decision, or to defer a decision, after weighing the available information and the likely consequences.

9 Action-oriented
Prefers to manage an active front-line operation where the challenges are concrete, varied, arise on the day and have immediate impact on the success of the enterprise; decisions demanded are immediate and often urgent.

10 Reflective
Prefers to manage a function where the work tends to be of like kind and the challenges can be forecast, analysed and reflected on; the impact of decisions is delayed.

II Interpersonal

11 Social impact
Manages others' impressions by projecting a positive image of him/herself.

12 Positive influencing
Has the desire and skill to move others willingly towards a desired goal or course of action.

169

13 Positive regard
Believes in and values others and respects their views and ideas.

14 Oral communication and presentation
Uses the spoken word and gesture to communicate thoughts effectively and convincingly, either in informal interactions or in formal presentations.

15 Responsive communication
Listens attentively to others in order to hear what they have to say and to understand fully the message behind the words.

16 Written communication
Expresses observations, ideas and arguments in written form so that they are readily understood and make the desired impression on the reader.

III Work and organisational experience

17 Resource management
Identifies and evaluates resourcing needs and organises the acquisition and deployment of people, plant, software, vehicles and equipment.

18 Control
Controls an operation or a business, monitoring indicators and taking corrective action in response to deviations from expectation or standard.

19 Delegation
Delegates to immediate subordinates according to their maturity and experience.

20 Managing the human resource
Assesses, selects, develops, trains and coaches others.

21 Business understanding
Understands revenue, costs, cost containment, financial controls, spending and profitability.

22 Managing upward
Maintains effective relations with boss and others in authority.

23 Managing horizontal relationships
Maintains effective relations with colleagues, members of a team or task force, or suppliers.

24 Managing subordinates
Maintains effective working relationships by being firm and respectful, providing whatever tools and resources they require to achieve the desired outputs.

25 Working interdependently
Maintains effective relationships across organisational boundaries.

26 Organisational understanding
Understands the forces, constraints and management systems and structures found in a _____ business.

27 Customer orientation
Habitually thinks of the needs of the customer, is responsive to the customer's requirements and complaints, can view services and products from customer's point of view.

28 Industry knowledge
Understands the operation, products, services, markets, market forces and other dimensions of the _____ industry.

29 Representing the organisation
Able and willing to represent the organisation to its best advantage to external people, bodies or the public.

30 Knowledge and understanding
Knows and understands overseas conditions such as _____ in _____ countries.

APPENDIX 4: REFERENCES AND FURTHER READING

Chapter 1 Why Assessment and Selection?

Arvey, R. D. *Fairness in Selecting Employees* Reading Mass: Addison–Wesley, 1979

Bedford, T. and Feltham, R. T. *A Cost Benefit Analysis of the Extended Interview*, Home Office Unit at CSSB, Report No. 2, 1986

Herriot, P. and Fletcher, C. 'Candidate-friendly selection for the 1990s', *Personnel Management* London: February 1990

Chapter 2 Starting with the Job and the Selection Criteria

O'Neill, B. 'Developing future leaders at British Airways', Devine, M. (ed.), *The Photofit Manager: Building a Picture of Management in the 1990s* London: Unwin Hyman, 1990

Parker, H. *Letters to a New Chairman* London: Institute of Directors, 1990

Pearn, M. and Kandola, R. S. *Job Analysis: A practical guide for managers* London: Institute of Personnel Management, 1987

Schneider, B. *Staffing Organisations* Santa Monica: Goodyear Publishing Company, 1976

Chapter 3 The Tools of Assessment

Bevan, S. and Fryatt, J. 'Employee Selection in the UK', Report No 160, Institute of Manpower Studies, University of Sussex, 1988

Herriot, P. (ed.) *Assessment and Selection in Organisations, Methods and Practice for Recruitment and Appraisal* Chichester: Wiley, 1989

Chapter 4 Organising the Assessment Programme

Drenth, P. and Algera, J. 'Personnel selection', Warr, P. (ed.) *Psychology at Work*, 3rd Edition London: Penguin, 1987

Smith, M. and Robertson, I. T. *Systematic Staff Selection* London: Macmillan Press, 1986

Chapters 5 and 6 Preparing for the Interview, and Making the Interview Work on the Day

Breakwell, G. *Interviewing* London: The British Psychological Society, 1990

Gratus, J. *Successful Interviewing: How to Find and Keep the Best People* London: Penguin Books, 1988

Herriot, P. 'The selection interview', Warr, P. (ed.) *Psychology at Work*, 3rd edn. London: Penguin, 1987

Chapter 7   Objective Testing in Personnel Selection

British Psychological Society *Principles governing the employment of psychological tests* Bulletin of the British Psychological Society, 1981, 34, 317–318

British Psychological Society *Principles governing the employment of psychological tests* Bulletin of the British Psychological Society, 1981, 34, 317–318

Downs, S. *Testing Trainability*, 1985 (Available through the ASE division of NFER Nelson)

Institute of Personnel Management *The IPM Code on Psychological Testing* IPM, 1989

Keyser, D. J. and Sweetland, R. C. Eds. *Tests: Second Edition* Kansas. Test Corporation of America, 1986 (Available through the ASE division of NFER Nelson)

Toplis, J., Dulewicz, V. and Fletcher, C. *Psychological Testing: A Practical Guide* London: Institute of Personnel Management, 1987

Chapter 8   Using Psychological Tests

Craig, M. 'Trainability and new technology in newspaper production', *News Review* of the Industrial Training Research Unit: March, 1989

Pearn, M. A., Kandola, R. S. and Mottram, R. D. *Selection Tests and Sex Bias* London: Equal Employment Commission, Published by HMSO, 1987

Chapter 9   Assessment and Development Centres

Dulewicz, V. 'Assessment Centres as the Route to Competence', *Personnel Management*, November 1989

Feltham, R. 'Assessment centres', in Herriot, P. (ed.) *Assessment and Selection in Organisations, Methods and Practice for Recruitment and Appraisal* Chichester: Wiley, 1989

Greatrex, J. 'BP's move from assessment to development', in Devine, M. (ed.), *The Photofit Manager: Building a Picture of Management in the 1990s* London: Unwin Hyman, 1990

'A quicker way up the promotion ladder', *Police Review*, 9 March, 1990

Reddy, M. *The Manager's guide to Counselling at Work* London: Methuen and The British Psychological Society, 1990

Stewart, A. M. and Stewart, V. *Tomorrow's Manager Today*, 2nd edn. London: Institute of Personnel Management, 1981

Thornton, C. G. and Byham, W. C. *Assessment Centers and Managerial Performance* New York: Academic Press, 1982

Chapter 10   Behind the Scenes

Georgiades, N. 'A strategic future for personnel?' *Personnel Management* February, 1990

Chapter 11 A Systematic Overview

British Psychological Society, *A Code of Conduct for Psychologists*, bulletin of the British Psychological Society, 1985, 38, 41–43

Coussey, M. and Whitmore, J. *Jobs and Racial Equality* Corby: British Institute of Management, 1986

Society for Industrial and Organisation Psychology *Principles for the Validation and Use of Personnel Selection Procedures*, 3rd edn. Maryland: University of Maryland, 1987

Wood, R. *Discrimination through Assessment*, unpublished report to the Manpower Services Commission, 1987

APPENDIX 5: USEFUL ADDRESSES

SUPPLIERS OF TESTS AND OTHER ASSESSMENT MATERIALS

There are many suppliers of which the following is a sample:

Psychological tests
1 ASE Division
NFER Nelson Publishing Company Ltd.
Darville House
2 Oxford Road East
Windsor
Berkshire SL4 1DF
Tel: 0753 850333

Assessment Centre exercises
2 DDI (UK) Ltd.
Keystone House
Boundary Road
Loudwater
High Wycombe HP10 9BY
Tel: 0628 810800

Psychological tests
3 EITS
Educational and Industrial Test
Services Ltd.
83 High Street
Hemel Hempstead
Hertfordshire HP1 3AH
Tel: 0442 56773

Psychological tests
4 Independent Assessment and
Research Centre
57 Marleybone Street
London W1N 3AE
Tel: 071 935 2373

Trainability tests
5 Industrial Training Research Unit
71 Bridge Street
Cambridge CB2 1UR
Tel: 0223 351576

Psychological tests
6 Knight Chapman Psychological Ltd.
48 High Street
Lewes BN7 2DD
Tel: 0273 471535

Psychological tests
7 Oxford Psychologists Press Ltd.
Lambourne House
311–321 Banbury Road
Oxford OX2 7JH
Tel: 0865 510203

Computer systems for selection
8 Pilat Ltd.
9 Wendover Court
Lyndale Avenue
London NW2
Tel: 071 431 4554

*Tests for programming and
word processing*
9 Psychometrics Ltd.
22 Peryn Road
London W37 NA
Tel: 071 746 2213

Psychological tests
10 SHL
Saville and Holdsworth Ltd.
The Old Post House
21 High Street
Esher, Surrey KT10 9QA
Tel: 0372 68634
and
4 Malone Road
Belfast
Tel: 0232 661616

Psychological tests
11 SRA
    Science Research Associates
    Newton Road
    Henley-on-Thames
    Oxfordshire RG9 1EW
    Tel: 0491 575959

Psychological tests
12 The Psychological Corporation
    Foots Cray
    High Street
    Sidcup DA14 5HP
    Tel: 081 300 1149

OCCUPATIONAL PSYCHOLOGISTS AND CONSULTANTS

There are many qualified practitioners of whom the following are a sample:

CPCR Human Resource Consultants
Eldon House
Regent Centre
Gosforth
Newcastle-upon-Tyne NE3 3PW
Tel: 091 2130990

Fletcher, Dulewicz and Associates
Premier House Suite 424
10 Greycoat Place
London SW1P 1SB
Tel: 071 674 1940

Innovation Management Consultants
3 Warwick Road
Hampton Wick
Kingston-upon-Thames
Surrey KT1 4DW
Tel: 081 977 6739

McKenzie Davey
16 Kent Terrace
Regents Park
London NW1 4RP
Tel: 071 724 0330

Pearn Kandola Downs
76 Banbury Rd.
Oxford OX2 6JT
Tel: 0865 516202

Psychometric Research & Development Ltd.
Brewmaster House
The Maltings
St Albans
Hertfordshire AL1 1NG
Tel: 0727 41455

Rothwell Douglas Ltd.
95 Brondesbury Road
London NW6 6RY
Tel: 071 624 0690

Team Focus Ltd.
Hawtrey House
12 Ray Park Avenue
Maidenhead
Berkshire SL6 8DS
Tel: 0628 37338

Walton Churchill Plc.
Brittanic House
32 High Street
Northwich
Cheshire CW9 5BL
Tel: 0606 48438

PROFESSIONAL BODIES

The British Psychological Society
St. Andrews House
48 Princess Road East
Leicester LE1 7DR
Tel: 0533 549568

The Institute of Personnel Management
IPM House
Camp Road
Wimbledon
London SW19 4UW
Tel: 071 946 9100

Index